THIS
WOMAN
CAN

The NO bullsh*t guide for women who lead

Janice Sutherland

Rights

The moral rights of the author have been asserted. No part of this book may be reproduced, stored in a retrieval system, or transmitted in any form, or by any means, electronic, photocopying, recording or otherwise, without the prior permission of the Author.

This book is sold subject to the condition that it shall not by way of trade or other be lent, re-sold, hired-out or otherwise circulated without the author's prior consent in any form of binding or cover other than in which it is published and without a similar condition including this condition being imposed upon the subsequent purchaser.

© Copyright Janice Sutherland 2018

Disclaimer

The material in this publication is of the nature of general comment only, and does not represent professional advice. It is not intended to provide specific guidance for particular circumstances, and it should not be relied upon as the basis for any decision to take action or not take action on any matter that it covers. Readers should obtain professional advice where appropriate, before making any such decision. To the maximum extent permitted by law, the author and publisher disclaim all responsibility and liability to any person, arising directly or indirectly from any person taking action or not taking action based on the information in this publication.

Acknowledgements

For Derrick, who has always believed me in, even when I was hard work.

To my boys – Jordan and Jake, who despite being grown will forever be my babies.

Thanks to Dee Hutchinson and the Deepartures gang, my virtual support team.

To the person who inspired my This Woman Can attitude – my mom Ruth Brotherson.

Contact Information

Whether she's working one-on-one with corporate executives, speaking to conference audiences, or conducting her This Woman Can programs, Janice Sutherland is inspiring female leaders everywhere.

If you are a conference or organization looking for a high-energy speaker/facilitator to engage and inspire, Janice is available to speak at women's and leadership conferences, corporate meetings and off-sites and conventions. As a coach, her organizational workshops relate to numerous topics including leadership presence, mastering resilience, leading with authenticity and high potential leadership development programs. Contact info@janicesutherland.com

To learn more about Janice's This Woman Can personal coaching programs and to claim your free online coaching program as a thank you for purchasing this book, visit: http://thiswomancan.coach.

Find out more about Janice Sutherland by joining her on any of the following social media pages

Follow me on at https://facebook.com/iamjanicesutherland

Follow me on Instagram
http://instagram.com/iamjanicesutherland

Connect with me on LinkedIn at
https://www.linkedin.com/in/iamjanicesutherland

What you will get from this book

Despite the growth in number of female leaders in business, diversity in the C-suite is still a huge challenge, even more so if you're a woman of color. This is not solely because of the patriarchal nature of the business environment but also because women get in their own way by not projecting the confidence to challenge societal expectations due to their own preconceived limitations.

In *This Woman Can*, author Janice Sutherland approaches relatable scenarios that both aspiring and existing female leaders face with candor, honesty and simplicity. Providing solutions for women to develop self-belief in their capabilities to becoming high performance leaders both at work and in their lives. Utilizing her personal knowledge as one of the Caribbean's first female CEOs in the male dominated telecommunications industry and drawing on her experiences as an executive leadership coach, she provides practical answers without bullshit acronyms that women can utilize to get the job done.

Sutherland opens the conversation surrounding thorny topics such as, dispelling the myth of work life balance, owning your career path, navigating the board room to the taboo subjects of being a female bread winner and having the confidence to say no to those who matter in order to achieve some sanity in your work and personal life. Each chapter provides concise bulleted applications and a list of self- reflection questions to consider that will guide women of all ages along the leadership pathway. As an added bonus, customers who purchase this book will receive access to an online coaching course valued at almost $300.

She demonstrates that with pragmatic approaches, women can break expectations if they believe in, own and confidently develop their personal power and not wait for empowerment.

If you put your mind to it – This Woman Can.

Contents

Introduction 13

1. This Woman Can... have the confidence to own her career move. 19

    You're just full of IT.... Excuses that is! 20

    No one is ever ready 20

    I don't know enough, I'll feel like a fraud 20

    Want to lead? – First, become a leader of YOU 21

    You are the only obstacle in your path 22

    You're worth it 22

    Procrastination, Overwhelm and Self-Sabotage 23

    You've got this! 23

    Don't fight the feeling 24

2. This Woman Can... successfully pivot in her career! 27

    The 10 Step Career Pivot 28

3. This Woman Can... return to her career 35

    Own Your Break 36

    Assess Your Situation 37

    Don't Wait to Be Found 38

    Be Confident and Prepared for Change 39

    Remember you have as much to offer 40

4. This Woman Can... set boundaries! 43

    Creating boundaries at work 43

    Creating boundaries with your partner 45

    Creating boundaries with your children 47

5. This Woman Can... give feedback without drama. 51
    The Four Step Feedback Approach (SBID).......................52
    Adding the friend dynamic 55

6. This Woman Can... navigate her relationship and her career...59

7. This Woman Can... believe that she earned her seat at the table...67

8. This Woman Can... be the main breadwinner. 73

9. This Woman Can... confidently navigate the Board Room! 79
    Before the meeting..80
    Self-Preparation 82
    During the meeting 84
    After the meeting 85
    This woman can self-reflection questions; 86

10. This Woman Can... say no, without damaging her career!...87
    So, what would could you do to make saying NO a little more comfortable?..87
    Don't fear the No!...88
    What happens if you keep saying yes? 88
    Should I Say No to The Boss? 89
    So How Do I say NO? 91

11. This Woman Can... not take things personally............95

12. This Woman Can... manage feeling overwhelmed. 101

13. This Woman Can... manage the office bully! 109

14. This Woman Can... be in control of her personal development...117

15. This Woman Can... believe she's good enough!........127

16. This Woman Can... exit gracefully! 133
17. This Woman Can... be strong enough to handle sexual harassment..143
18. This Woman Can... fight the fear of leadership! 151
19. This Woman Can... have a courageous conversation! 161

    Preparation 162

20. This Woman Can... integrate life and work!..............167

    Control the beast called Work! 173

21. This Woman Can... proactively support other women. 179

About the Author..187

Introduction

I was never any good at playing small - my dad would say "mek you self small" when he had to pile six children and two adults into his Ford Cortina 1600 E (the E was very important). As the eldest of six children, I'm not sure if I was born with the leadership gene or if it was thrust upon me just because of sheer circumstances.

The last of the Baby Boomer Generation, eldest child and a product of Caribbean Island parents, becoming a CEO "back home" wasn't the career path you aspired to. Instead you may have followed your parents into the factory, drove a bus or become a nurse. There's nothing wrong with any of those roles, but I just knew that after feeling like I worked in a factory (cooking meals for the family), being in charge of the walking school bus (you're the eldest and you all go to the same school so you're responsible for all of you getting there and returning home), play nursing (caring for every sick sibling so mum could go to work). I wanted something different and I was lucky to have a progressive mother who wanted more for me too, but it still wasn't becoming a leader in multi-cultural Britain!

She allowed me to break the norm and become the first in our family to go off to college. Unfortunately, my future plans were interrupted by life which had other ideas and after a teenage marriage, I was in my late twenties, a societal cliché - a single parent with two children, a divorcee, and an abused ex-wife with very little career prospects. Having to face some very difficult situations with more difficult decisions to be made for both my life,career and those of my children.

So, like I said, I was never very good at playing small and set myself the challenge of getting answers to the following questions;

- What were my goals and aspirations and who could I talk to about them?
- What would it take for me to really believe that I was more than who I am at that moment?
- What had I always wanted to do but had never given myself permission to do?
- What had I been telling myself I couldn't do but hadn't tried?
- What was my plan to attain my aspirational goals?

These five questions formed and continue to be the basis of how I approach my career as I realized that I had to invest in my personal growth, by committing to my education, invest in mentors, training and resources to help me get to the next level. I understood that I'd stagnate in my career, if I didn't reach for new tools and learn more to fully deliver my potential. So, I went back to school, I challenged my personal beliefs every day by taking every opportunity to learn never accepting that it couldn't be done - from becoming the first black parent governor at my children's school, being the first woman to attain a Masters in Strategic Sales, proactively seeking mentors within each organization I worked and running two marathons.

This approach has rewarded me well as over the past 25 years. I've held senior leadership roles across many industries and held a position where I was fortunate to become the first female CEO for a telecommunications company in the Caribbean managing multi-million-dollar business' spanning two countries. My career culminating as a leadership and executive coach, where I've had the opportunity to coach some fabulous women both professionally and as a mentor.

Why This Woman Can?

As I pursued leadership positions, I had a hard time finding female role models and more importantly those who also looked like me, ones that I could really connect to. I loved wearing the corporate suit and high heels, absolutely adored and could rock shocking pink, however my leadership style was in no way the uber bland corporate approach the male dominated environment expected. I wasn't frivolous or masculine - I stayed true to me. I'd already spent a significant amount of time conforming in a bad marriage - I refused to let that follow me into my corporate life.

I realized that to get ahead I couldn't rely solely on merit - I would be just a name in a multitude of names. I had to be seen doing a great job - be highly visible and build strategic relationships with those in decision-making roles. Yes, this woman could and did!

In coaching sessions and employee one to ones I would often hear of the struggles women faced not only as they navigated the leadership career ladder but also the impact leadership roles placed on their personal lives. These were not just women who were embarking on their corporate careers but also experienced women in established leadership roles who despite their success, still suffered with low confidence and bouts of self-doubt, feeling they were still having to prove themselves in the board room or other male dominated environs.

All these learning experiences have taught me that although women have more choice on how they show up in their leadership, the same challenges I faced over 30 years ago are still prevalent today;

- Limited female role models within the leadership realm.

- Lack of self-belief and confidence in our competencies
- Struggling with our authenticity - embarrassed to lead with our true selves.
- Really getting past the feeling of being an impostor and taking ownership of our achievements.
- Having the confidence to reach out and accept help without seeing it as a sign of weakness.

Which is where **This Woman Can** comes in. I'm a huge believer in "paying it forward' so, this book is part memoir, part experiential and part coach, capturing learnings from all the "real talk" conversations I've participated in as an executive coach and my own societal defying experiences as I rose to become a successful CEO on my own terms.

I share the scenarios working women grapple with continuously but fear vilification if they reveal how they truly feel or seek advice. Sometimes anxiety and uncertainty, sometimes crises of confidence but often annoying frustration that they had to deal with the situations presented. Coupled with exhilaration and sense of accomplishment once they applied their coaching actions, the confirmation that they could execute their role as good as any man in similar positions.

It is a pragmatic "how to" guide for the common situations women encounter, those times when we just want a real answer to our real challenges not text book acronyms. It's "snackable" reading material as we're all busy and don't have time to wade through tomes of information, so use this Janicefesto to solve the challenges we can all face from time to time.

This isn't about empowering women, empowered by definition means" authority or power given to someone to do something". Women i.e. YOU already have the power, you just need to trust in your abilities, unleash them and believe THIS WOMAN CAN.

1. This Woman Can... have the confidence to own her career move.

I had been coaching Regina, for three months. She was smart, driven, successful and on the fast track for promotion in her current company. We had been working together to improve her leadership skills, board room confidence and ready her for the new executive role we knew she was destined for. That opportunity presented itself and I was delighted for her, she'd worked hard to get recognized and demonstrate that she could step up to a senior role. However, Regina was not so happy, and our next session went something like this;

"I'm not ready"

"I don't think I'm ready"

"I'm unsure if I'm ready"

"I need to learn A, B, C first"

"It's not the right time"

"Maybe in the future"

Can you relate to Regina's experience? Have you ever looked at or been presented with a great opportunity and felt tremendously excited AND hopelessly inadequate all at the same time, convinced that you're not ready, just like Regina?

The goal in this situation is not to focus on why you're not ready but to focus on all the reasons why you are – after all you've worked for this!

You're just full of IT…. Excuses that is!

It's all an excuse! But the fact that you feel nervous, concerned, and even distressed about the new path you're embarking on is a good sign! This type of stress is great, as it provides you with enough productive discomfort to grow and stretch yourself.

As a coach it's my role to help you understand what's stopping you from feeling ready and supporting you, so you can start your incredible journey as opposed to just thinking ifs, buts and maybes.

No one is ever ready

Very few people wake up with the ambition of being a leader, the question whether a leader is born or created is on ongoing debate. What I can tell you is that regardless of nature or nurture you will always be learning. You never stop; so waiting until you believe you are ready and feeling sorry for yourself is a waste of your valuable time. Sorry is a comfort to a fool (to take one of my Mom's favorite sayings). What you need is the desire to be a leader after that, you do, you make mistakes and you learn, you do, you make mistakes and you learn, you do, you make mistakes and you learn. You see the pattern?

I don't know enough, I'll feel like a fraud

The key word is feel and it's a feeling most of us know well. Your boss commends you after a report you submitted and the first thing that comes to your mind is "I hope they don't find out I'm not as great as they think I am." Or being offered a promotion, and thinking to yourself "How long before they see that I actually don't deserve this – I'm such a fraud".

Each of us may have our own version, but the essence of it is that you feel like an impostor. That's what imposter syndrome is. Women tend to feel it more than men – often because we are wired to not think of ourselves as leaders, innovators, and business warriors... the kinds of self-imagery men are exposed to from a young age. This has nothing to do with readiness or any knowledge that you think you may be lacking; instead this is the fear of inadequacy and 'impostor syndrome'. You feel that you are not good enough, wise enough, and knowledgeable to become a leader and therefore you feel you cannot get started. To repeat myself, the only way to get over this is "you do, you make mistakes and you learn". When you learn you will feel competent, when you feel competent you will develop your confidence. Your results will give you the reassurance and evidence that you need to know that you are more than enough and tell you what you need to do next.

Want to lead? – First, become a leader of YOU

Think about this, how did you get to where you are now? You weren't born knowing everything that you know now. You gained knowledge from your experiences, people around you, the education system and various methods of knowledge acquisition, that's what got you to where you are currently. You probably weren't consciously aware of how or what you were learning, how to interpret it, when to use said knowledge. Being grown, we have a habit of over thinking which sabotages our ability to learn and apply. Yet as a child we just got on with things, without much thought. We 'believe' that we have to acquire all the 'new things' that we need to learn before we take any action, how absurd is that?

This is you being led by a false assumption, don't fall into this thought process. Be the leader of your own thoughts, what is it that you want to do and if you are not doing it why haven't you started?

You are the only obstacle in your path

Yes, you are the product of your experiences, interactions with other people and through conscious development you have chosen experiences that manage your perception in a way that benefits you. You might have had things that have happened to you, things you could not control. However, the one thing that you can control is yourself. Your mind is your greatest and most powerful asset. When you tell yourself you're not ready, it can be as a result of the perceptions you've created because of said interactions but it doesn't have to be. So, if there is something holding you back, embrace it, face it and if needed get help and assistance.

You're worth it

As women we're often guilty of putting everyone else ahead of us, children, significant other, friends etc. but investing in yourself may be the most profitable investment you ever make. It yields not only future returns, but often a current pay-off as well. The surest way to achieve a better-quality life, to be successful, productive and satisfied, is to place a priority on investing in both personal and professional growth. The effort you put into consistently investing in yourself plays a large role in determining the quality of your life now and in the future.

Procrastination, Overwhelm and Self-Sabotage

Procrastination, Overwhelm and Self-Sabotage (POS) are three evils that will lead you to your downfall. Experiencing POS ultimately leads you to feeling unfulfilled and dissatisfied with yourself and how your life is. You will feel frustrated and the spiral of negative thought only continues to spiral downwards.

When you are experiencing it, it's vital that you don't ignore it, get to the root of the problem and do something about it. If not tackled now, it will follow you all the way through your leadership journey, impacting your decisions, making you second guess yourself. Self-improvement and change only comes from taking action.

You've got this!

Fight the fear! You have everything you need to take the first step towards becoming a great leader. One of the best ways to get over your fear of not being ready is by actually doing the thing that you fear the most. Exposing yourself to your fear (and gradual increase of exposure) can help alleviate fear and anxiety around the feeling of unreadiness! When you fear you won't perform 'well enough' or 'perfectly' do it anyway. This in turn, will help to boost your self-esteem and identity.

Focus, on one step at a time. Each step, no matter how small will have an impact, each step effects change. You know yourself best, so be productive, it's your race so you can set your own pace.

Don't fight the feeling

The level of feeling ready can vary for everyone but here is the truth about what will make you start feeling ready:

- No longer assuming that you're not ready.
- No longer turning your back to the fact that you are ready.
- No longer trying to find evidence that you are ready.

They may sound similar, but they are different statements that are powerful if you answer them honestly. Get your thoughts out of your head and onto paper, video or voice record it, do whatever works for you.

Remember one thing: everyone started somewhere and probably felt unready at some time in their life. It's normal. But you don't want to have to deal with the fear of not being ready for the rest of your life. Take charge by figuring out how you can battle this thought and challenge yourself to step up.

This woman can self-reflection questions

- What's preventing you from being excited about new opportunities?
- How does this opportunity align with your values?
- If you knew you'd succeed, what would you do?
- What would be possible if you weren't censoring yourself?
- What evidence do you have that supports your readiness?

- On a scale of 1 to 10, how committed are you to make this move? If lower, what would make it a 10?

"**Behind every successful woman is someone who believes in her,
who has the confidence that she can achieve her dreams.
That person is herself.**"
Anon.

2. This Woman Can... successfully pivot in her career!

Patricia was a lifer!

Not in prison but with her job.

When we first started our coaching relationship, she'd been in her role as shift supervisor for 7 years and had been with her current company for 20 years. She had an exemplary record but felt that despite voicing her career aspirations in her annual reviews, applying and being turned down for more senior roles, she felt her employers still viewed her in a limited capacity and she had become a victim of her own success. After all, if she was doing a great job why move her?

During our discussions, Patricia realized that if she wanted more seniority, she would have to consider working another for organization. This thought paralyzed her into "in action". In her eyes, she was no longer the carefree 25-year-old she had been when she embarked on her career, she couldn't just pivot into a new job and compete with the other Baby Boomers and let's not forget the mass of millennials;

- She had responsibilities.
- She was scared of the unknown.
- She was nauseated with overwhelm.
- She was unsure if her current knowledge would help with her future aspirations.

I assured her that these were common and valid feelings which meant we would have to embark on a plan that would will give her the best chance of succeeding with her career change – The 10 Steps of The Career Pivot!

The 10 Step Career Pivot

1. **Consider your transferable skills.**

   These are the skills you've gained throughout your career, additionally they can include your volunteer work, hobbies, sports, and other life experiences. Analyze your current skills and consider how they might be transferable. Someone with an executive background, for example, already understands HR, legal and marketing. Can they can be used in your next job or career without any further refinement? Identify and understand your gaps. Ask yourself: What do I know? What skills and experiences do I have? What do I need for the next step? What are your strengths? What drives you, what makes you "tick"? They may bring an entirely different skillset to the fore.

2. **Understand Your Personal Brand**

   Recognize that you have a reputation within your personal and professional lives. That reputation, combined with your skillsets and strengths is your personal brand. Understanding your personal brand is a great way to make a successful career pivot. More than just your appearance, your personal brand speaks to others about who you are, what you are known for and how you add value to any situation. Take some time out to really understand your personal brand, as it requires self-reflection and lots of effort on your part, but it will pay dividends in the end.

3. **Embrace the Fear.**

   Fear is often a key reason that keeps people from changing, we worry about what will happen if we change jobs and don't like the role? If we're embarking on the entrepreneurial route how will we earn enough to take care of ourselves, our family without a regular income? We worry that we might fail in the next role.

   Embrace the fear, it's a sign that you're excited at making a change. Manage the fear by taking control of the steps in the change process, make sure you've done your homework, your research, you have clarity as to what the next move is, have you challenged your personal rationale for making the change? There are no guarantees even in your current role but at least you'll know you've done everything to enable a smooth transition.

4. **Consider is it your actual role, the industry or the company you work for?**

   Early in our career, we may have taken the first job we were offered as the appeal of actually earning was too good to pass up or we were scared we wouldn't get a better offer. If you like your current field and know where you want to transition to, then start some serious investigation. Use online networking sites such as LinkedIn to see which people have similar roles, what industries they work in that may appeal. Reach out to your physical network, these maybe people you know in your field, attend industry networking events, have informal chats to people in roles that appeal, ask them how they got into the industry, what's unique to the organization? If you want to move into a totally new field, can you find a sponsor e.g. a former colleague in your new field who will hire you and teach you the ropes?

5. Feel like you want to go it alone?

Do you have a side hustle? It's a great way to test the waters, I started my coaching practice whilst working full-time, I wanted to know that a) I could attract clients and b) it would be something I'd want to do full time. It's all well and good doing the hustle part-time but when it becomes your financial cushion you have to make sure it's both sustainable and will hold your interest. So, if you're a writer, photographer or into making jewelry, clothing etc., what are the ways you could ply your trade whilst still in full time work? Could you sell items on EBay or Etsy? Could you take photos at children's parties? Make sure entrepreneurship is for you before you take the plunge.

6. Unsure what your next move is?

Know you need a change but don't know where to start? I'm a big believer that even adults need career counselling, so consider talking to a coach who can guide you through the questions you need to consider. Alternatively, open your heart and mind to the unknown. When you're feeling lost, being open to new possibilities means you're more likely to stumble upon something that makes your heart flutter. There are plenty of options to explore new skills, evening classes, and free online courses by sites such as Alison. Taking a class or workshop can quickly tell you if that might make for a satisfying career shift and it doesn't always mean spending hundreds of dollars on university courses.

7. **Love the job but not the hours?**

   There was a time in the past when "freelance" was code for "can't handle a real job" but the world has changed, thanks to millennials—most of whom will have had multiple jobs before they're 30. If you want to move from project to project and control everything from your hours to your hourly rate, you no longer have to worry about losing reputation. If you want to transition to freelance work, make sure you keep your network intact and maintain relationships—these can prove to be invaluable for work and if you ever need to return to a more stable atmosphere. Make sure you have the basics to market your skills: a simple website, an updated LinkedIn profile, and a public resume, depending on your field. Then go out there and tell your network that you're going freelance, ask people what they need, and how you can help them achieve it.

8. **Don't listen to the naysayers but do have the right expectations.**

   If you're about to leave your job, enter a new industry or embark on a totally different journey, be aware that your career change will likely result in some trade-offs: primarily a hit to both your finances and your ego. Make sure you understand what you're getting yourself into. Be prepared to work incredibly hard, be patient and realistic as to what the move entails both once you're in or looking for a new role. Get into the mindset that you are/will become a brand-new employee. Be fluid and opportunistic.

9. **Do have the right conversations.**

   People including your loved ones will question your decisions and your sanity for the change. Make sure you talk to them and gain their support or at least their understanding (you can agree to disagree) but bottom line it's your decision!

10. **Remember when all is said and done, it's your decision.**

    All that really matters is that you've made peace with your decisions, as in the end no one can live your life other than you. Most of all, don't give up! Do something you love. Life is too short to be stuck in a job that doesn't fulfill you.

Completing the plan took three months, during which we saw a lot of tears but more importantly I saw growth in Patricia's confidence and her ability to step out of her comfort zone.

This woman can self-reflection questions;

- If you could spend the rest of your life doing the most amazing thing you've ever dreamed of, what would it be?
- What jobs would allow you to do the most amazing thing?
- What obstacles stand in your way?
- What life and professional experiences do you already possess that would equip you for your next career?
- What new experiences or skills might help you reach your career goals?
- How could you leverage your network to find the best fit?
- What's one small step you could take to explore the possibilities in this new career?

"A strong woman is a woman determined to do something others are determined cannot be done."
Marge Piercy

3. This Woman Can... return to her career.

Roxanne had taken the decision to move back into the corporate world, after the last of her two children had commenced school. She was nervous, as even though she'd supported her husband's business on a part-time basis she hadn't worked for an external organization for over two years. Her concern was that even though she'd previously held senior positions she wouldn't be able to compete with the millennials or no one would take her return to corporate life seriously. More importantly, she didn't want to start at bottom of the ladder, as she had 7–8 years management experience.

"Janice" she said, "How do I return to work after my career break?"

When I took the decision to move away from corporate life and embark on my entrepreneurial journey establishing my own leadership development business, it was a calculated choice and I was fortunate to be a position to plan my transition. However, it can be nerve racking when you have to return to work after being at the top of your career, maybe you were on a forced break due pregnancy, illness or you just needed to step away, take a career break.

My research indicates that the four most common reasons for women quitting their jobs are marriage, relocation, childbirth and caring for the elderly, and the breaks can range from 6 months to 15 years. An unplanned career break can spell disaster for most professionals and unfortunately, many women who interrupt their careers for personal reasons, do so without a plan in mind. Without an end date, a break can stretch much longer than desirable.

Whatever the motives you had for taking a career break, finding a job can be daunting enough, but it can be even more unnerving once you've taken a break from work. You may you feel anxious about starting a new job or you may worry that your skills are a little rusty because a lot has changed since you've been away from the workplace. US studies indicate that 70% of women fear taking a career break. From my experience coaching female executives, I know that many can suffer with a lack of confidence, feel out of touch with what's been going on in the corporate world they put on pause and have convinced themselves that it's impossible to find a satisfying corporate role after taking time out. It can be especially daunting when you're returning as a leader.

If you feel you're in this situation, here are some effective tips to help you increase your chances of stepping back into following a career break;

Own Your Break

It's quite common for a woman to believe that a gap on their resume or will ruin their career chances. However, don't view it as a handicap, see it as something positive that can differentiate you from other candidates. You'll have a hard-enough job trying to mask the break especially if you've not been working for a long period of time, so don't try to hide it. A break can offer lots of benefits that can make you just as an attractive hire, if not more so.

If you've had a long break, you'll likely have to discuss it within your cover letter, as well as during interviews. No matter what your reason for your extended leave from the workforce, keep your explanation brief.

Think of all the new skills you may have developed during your break, and explain how these can relate to the role you're now applying for. For example, did you take a course specializing in new technology? Conduct volunteer work and develop your leadership skills, which will help you to lead a team more effectively? Write a list of all of the jobs you have ever done, and for each of them identify what you enjoyed, felt challenged by, disliked and what provided the most work satisfaction. Look for patterns – were there any particular skills or roles that stood out as ones you loved? Or ones you really didn't enjoy? Pay attention to anything you learn about yourself, and use it to inform the type of roles you look for. Be prepared to address the questions that may arise;

- What did you learn about the industry during your downtime? What about yourself?
- What did it teach you about your goals and priorities? How do those relate to the position you're after?

By taking time to consider these questions and reframing your personal pitch, you'll be well on your way to feeling more comfortable and confident explaining your gap during your job search."

Whatever your reason for being away, try to distil it down to something brief—and the return the conversation to the work you did prior to your time away. Your work experience remains relevant, even if some time has passed since you gained that experience.

Assess Your Situation

Many women make the mistake of jumping straight back into the first job they can find believing that this is it, so I better not risk turning it down. Let's be honest, if you're not sure about a job, the interviewer may sense your uncertainty and will be unlikely to take you further in the hiring process. As a leader you've probably conducted a fair number of interviews, so you know the signs yourself.

If you're fortunate to secure a job that isn't right for you, you might even find yourself job hopping frequently before you find the right one – that in itself causes added complexity to your interview process. My advice, it's important to take some time to really assess your situation first and decide what you want to do. Talk to a coach, former colleagues or close friends, keeping an open your mind, remember, what was right for you before your career break, may not be the best fit for you now.

Don't Wait to Be Found

Now is not the time to be passive! In order to make a career change or tweak your role you need to get out there and start changing things for yourself. So, once you are clear of the direction you want to take,

- Start talking to people, offering your services, commenting, attending suitable events etc., don't forget to use your existing connections. Spend some time reaching out to your previous colleagues, clients, friends and family. Let them know that you're seeking a new position. Just be more visible

- Staying connected via LinkedIn or other social media platforms will also help keep you ahead of the curve in the long run. Subscribe to industry magazines, blogs and newsletters to further arm yourself with industry knowledge.

- If you haven't done so already, get your LinkedIn profile up to date (or edit it to ensure it shows you up in the best possible light). Then connect with ex-colleagues, friends and any other potentially useful acquaintances. If someone may be useful, send them a message and ask them if they can help you. If they know someone who needs your skills, they may also be happy to refer you.

- Work on your personal brand and be clear what you will say when asked "Tell me about yourself?" and "what made you decide to return to work?" and "what is your value now?" These opening lines are vital. Practice your responses endlessly with your coach, friends, failing that video them.

Be Confident and Prepared for Change

Whether you've been away from work for 10 months or 10 years, getting back into the leadership realm can be nerve-racking. However, the most important thing is that you remain confident in your abilities. Without confidence, you can easily undervalue what you can offer as a leader. No matter how well you prepare, taking a sabbatical means there will be changes. When you return to work, be ready to take on a few challenges before you settle back in;

- You may feel you lack credibility having not managed or led people in a while, but credibility is built over time, just trust in your abilities.

- Once you are offered a role, don't devalue yourself make sure that you pitch yourself at the right salary and charge proper rates for the specialist service or product that you provide, having been out of the game doesn't make you less valuable.

- Try not to worry about what other people expect of you, or their assumptions about what you 'should' do. And instead focus on what you want. It's all too easy to get caught in a people-pleasing trap, or to adhere to others' expectations of what you can do, and ignore the voice inside you that says, 'But this is not what I want!'

But pursuing a role you're not a perfect fit for, or that doesn't fire you up isn't good for you or your career long term. So, listen to your own instincts, and apply for the kind of positions that will stretch you and fulfil your needs and passions.

Remember you have as much to offer

Don't ever apologize for taking a break. It's not necessary and it will undermine you. Remember that women returning to the workplace add value and bring fresh thinking and a mature perspective.

This woman can self-reflection questions;

- What skills and experiences have you learnt/maintained that can ready you for your ideal position?
- How would you explain your career gap to a prospective employer and how does it make you a more competitive candidate for the role?
- What was your motivation for taking a career break?
- How do you know that you are now ready to return into full-time employment?
- How have you readied yourself to return to work?
- Who could you talk to who has been in a similar position i.e. taken a career break?
- Who in your network could you talk about potential opportunities?
- Assuming you know which career, you would like to return to,

- o What changes have you seen in the industry?
- o What skill/knowledge gaps (if any) do you have pertaining to your ideal role?
- o What is you plan to close the skill/knowledge gaps?

"It's a time to immerse yourself in a different environment, try new things, reassess your priorities, and look at your life from a different perspective."
Marelisa Fabrega

4. This Woman Can... set boundaries!

There was a time I really, really struggled with setting my personal boundaries and if you know me you'd be shaking your head in disbelief because this Janice is a misnomer. It's true, I allowed another to invade my physical and emotional space. I prioritized their needs and in turn, denied my own. I paid the consequence for allowing my boundaries to be blurred in that I became detached from myself, losing my integrity and authenticity along the way. It took a while to get back to me, but I had to break physically, emotionally and mentally before I realized I'd reached my absolute limit.

You don't have to go through that, at its core, boundary work involves self-care at the deepest level. Practicing healthy boundaries is a powerful way to practice self-love and acceptance, both inward and outward. To survive at the top in the corporate environment, boundary setting is a necessary practice that requires commitment and cultivation. Creating stronger boundaries is the number one way for most women to improve their lives.

Creating boundaries at work

With your boss - Sometimes bosses just don't understand boundaries. They call and text 24/7, email you in the middle of the night, and basically make you feel like you're working non-stop. And, unfortunately, they might need a sit-down conversation for you to tell them how you feel. Kindly let your boss know you love your job, but you also need to make sure you have some balance for your mental health — then ask if they have any suggestions on how to make that possible. If you don't let them know something is bothering you, they're never going to change (see Chapter 10. This Woman Can..... say no, without damaging her career!)

With your subordinates - It can be a challenge defining your professional boundaries at work especially if you've risen through the ranks to become a leader. That's just one type of the myriad of relationships you could be faced with in the professional environment. When I became CEO, a number of my peers became my subordinates and probably knew more about me personally than I would have shared had I joined them as their Boss from the get-go. It was a transition we'd all have to go through!

As a leader, I'm an open, determined and passionate person and I care for the people who work with (not for) me a great deal. As their boss it's my responsibility to be dependable, approachable and create a safe-feeling environment for the people who work with me. Employees perform at their best when they feel safe, so in short successful work boundaries equates to three main components: consistency, respect, and clear-cut expectations.

As a leader, your responsibility is to not surprise your employees with irrational behavior – they should know what you want from them and what the business needs. They should be regularly updated should things change. The standard you set for the rules of the office should apply to everyone (exceptions should be that – exceptions). You should be consistent about your expectations and the consequences if those expectations are not met. Treat everybody with dignity and respect; don't get caught up in office politics; be thoughtful and considerate and don't try to show off how important you are; spend time giving feedback to your direct reports weekly; listen to them and take and address their concerns seriously and you can't really go wrong. Understand that most employees are not unreasonable, they just need to feel understood and seen.

Creating boundaries with your partner

In my experience, saying no within a relationship can be achallenging concept but when achieved a healthy idyll.

We often take the stance that less disagreement equals less conflict and some couples don't even get that far. They just have a hard time voicing their opinions or needs altogether.

But saying yes, all the time when you don't really mean it, can actually be damaging for your relationship. It can build resentment, you may also become enmeshed as a couple and less of your own person.

Creating relationship boundaries are essential for any healthy relationship but tend to get a bad reputation as they're viewed as keeping partners away from each other. But it's just the opposite. Boundaries help you better understand your partner, know their needs and respond to them – thereby bringing you that much closer.

Denise was struggling with letting her partner know about how she felt about his "welcome home after your business trip" ritual.

"Every time I get home from a work trip Michael gets incredibly amorous – I know he misses me but after a few days of back to back meetings and the travel home, all I want to do is kick up my feet and chill. When I say no, he takes umbrage and I feel miserable as he takes it as rejection. Heck, I just need a couple of hours to catch myself – it's not a measure of how much I missed him"

It's a common scenario and one we regularly struggle to address as we fear hurting our significant other's feelings. The great news is it doesn't have to be that way, the alternative approach is that you sit down and talk with your other half about how you feel and agree that you need some time when you get home, maybe to unwind and get in the mood, let him set the scene etc., let him know how much you still want him but you need a little me time first, then you can both feel better.

If you don't address the divide, you'll just continue to feel bad, it'll chip away at your self-esteem, your husband will be none the wiser and you just keep getting upset.

You setting a boundary isn't the same as saying no to your relationship. It demonstrates that you care about your relationship and it's not all about work. You're saying no to a specific idea or event, and you should feel comfortable to open up when something negatively affects your well-being or sense of self, the same goes for your partner. When having the conversation, it's important to talk about your boundaries with "love, care and empathy," and only have discussions when you're both calm, not when you're on the verge of a blazing row, if your conversation is escalating, step back and take some time to consider how you can improve your talk.

Make sure you give a definite NO - Don't say "I'll think about it" if you don't want to do it. You'll just be dragging it out and make you feel even more stressed and the other person a level of expectation that they can ask again.

Remember that you deserve to have your own — and different — opinion and to voice it, articulating a different point of view doesn't mean you're asserting that you're better than your partner; it means you're not less.

So, saying no is a way of nurturing and empowering yourself and it encourages your partner to do the same, which in turn creates good will. Neither of you feels taken advantage of and you can both focus on practicing good self-care.

Creating boundaries with your children

Clarice's face burst onto my screen and she looked a little worse for wear. Her hair was out of its normally neat braided style, her eyes were tired, and she even looked irritated.

"Hey Clarice, you're not looking your normal self, what's up?"

"I feel really guilty and please forgive me for saying this, but there are just days I don't like my kids and today is one of those days. They are getting on my last ever nerve!

I'd promised to take the kids to the movies but haven't been able to do it and now they're pushing my buttons. Sometimes, it's so hard being an only parent with no-one to share the load. I feel so guilty having to stay late at work being and not being there when they need me, and they know it."

I'd heard this lament so many times not just from single parents but from married couples who work and even stay at home moms. First things first, I reassured her "Just because you don't like you're kids today, doesn't mean you love them any less - it's natural" I laughed.

"Kids aren't meant to be your best friend; their job is to push you are far as they can to get what they want but you're the one who sets boundaries!"

So much of why parents struggle to say "no" is because of other people's opinions or pressure from friends, family, or society in general. As parents we can often feel that we should do this, or we should allow that. Just stop comparing yourselves to others—or to an imagined ideal—and stop fearing being judged - people outside aren't raising your kids. You have to do what you think is right for your family.

The truth is nobody knows your values and your child better than you do, so try to remind yourself of that when you're feeling that outside pressure to be a certain way. Keep your focus on the big picture and remember: no matter the reason, giving in to your child is a "quick fix" that will almost guarantee problems later on.

Saying no is not cruel. Some parents would disagree, perhaps saying that you should reason with your child, explain yourself, or even negotiate. But avoid saying no, they urge, for fear that it will make your child feel resentful.

True, the word "no" might initially disappoint your child. Nevertheless, it teaches them a vital lesson—that in the real world, there are limits by which people must abide. By giving in, on the other hand, you weaken your authority and teach your child to manipulate you by whining every time he/she wants something. Over time, your response could make him/her resentful. After all, how much can a child respect an easily manipulated parent?

Your saying no prepares a child for adolescence and adulthood. It teaches them the benefits of self-denial. A child who learns that valuable lesson is less likely to give in during adolescence when he faces pressure to take drugs or to have premarital sex.

Your saying no also trains a child for adulthood. "The truth is, we [adults] don't always get what we want," We're not doing our kids any favors when we teach them that the world will always serve up whatever they want when they want it."

Ask yourself, 'What's the best thing to do for my child right now?'" Sometimes the answer is to set limits and give a consequence in order to teach them an important lesson about behavior.

Sometimes your child simply will not take no for an answer. Whenever you say the word, their unruly response tests your patience to the limit. Nothing you do or say calms them, and eventually you feel that you have no choice but to give in. Once again, your resolute no turns into an exasperated, reluctant yes.

Fabulous news, you can stop that tiresome pattern by;

1. **Focusing on your goal** - You want your child to become a competent, emotionally mature, successful adult. But you work against that objective if you give them everything they ask for. Saying no, therefore, is part of effective discipline. Such training will help your child, not hurt them

2. **Standing your ground** - When you say no, be decisive. Your child is not your equal, you are the adult, and they are your child. So, there is no need to debate your no as if you need them to approve it. Of course, as children grow, they need to have their "powers of discernment trained to distinguish both right and wrong." So, it is not wrong to reason with a child. Just don't forget the balance of power and don't get entangled in endless disputes with younger children about why you said no. The more you dispute with your child, the more your no will sound like a question rather than a decision.

3. **Accepting that your patience will be tested** - When done, stick to your decision. Your child might test your patience with whining or pleading. If that happens at home, what can you do? "Separate yourself from the child," Say, 'If you're in a whiny mood, that's OK, but I don't want to hear it. You need to go to your room.

You can whine there until you are ready to stop.'" At first, such a firm stance might be difficult for you to take—and for your child to accept. But their resistance is likely to lessen as they realize that you mean what you say.

4. **Stop flexing your parental muscle** – Just because you can, be reasonable, let your reasonableness become known. There are times when you can say yes to your child—as long as you are not giving in to mere whining and your child's request is legitimate.

There are many areas where you can face boundary challenges, but the connection is often a need to people please, but the upshot is 'We teach people how to treat us' and remember that your self-worth does not depend on how much you do for other people. Understand the importance of setting boundaries. Start setting boundaries in your relationships and watch the quality of them improve.

This woman can self-reflection questions;

- What areas of your life would benefit from stronger boundaries?
- What would it cost you if things remain the way they are?
- What actions could you take that would lessen the number of times that lead to you saying no?

"When we fail to set boundaries and hold people accountable, we feel used and mistreated.
This is why we sometimes attack who they are, which is far more hurtful than addressing a behavior or a choice."
Brené Brown

5. This Woman Can... give feedback without drama.

Mary had recently become a team manager and had transitioned from being responsible solely for herself to managing a team of ten diverse individuals. It was her first leadership role and she was quite rightly excited. We had agreed that the best way for me to support her, was to focus on improving her leadership skills during our coaching sessions. For this session she came armed with a situation she was finding challenging.

"How do you give feedback to someone that was previously your colleague, especially when it's negative? I don't want it to affect our personal relationship, but she has to respect that at work I'm her boss"

It's never easy giving feedback, especially when it's of the negative kind. You start getting tense, you run through all the reactionary scenarios in your mind (including the one where you Kung Fu kick the recipient in an effort to protect yourself).

Providing feedback is one of the most important skills for us to possess and whilst we think feedback is sacrosanct to leaders, it's a valuable skill to possess at any level. Yet, most people would rather have all their teeth removed without anaesthetic than sit down with an employee or loved one to address an issue. And because it's so uncomfortable, there are many times we simply "let things go" until the issues become intolerable and we blow! However, in the business environment, this is not good leadership behavior and creates liability for the organization if we don't address employee issues early on. Whilst in a personal relationship it just breeds resentment and a not so healthy partnership.

Unfortunately, not everyone embraces feedback as being a gift and sometimes just having the conversation can create conflict, defensiveness and drama. For this reason, most persons procrastinate in having these critical conversations. However, the biggest reason people get defensive is because of how crudely the feedback message is delivered. Without the right approach or proper tone of voice, the conversation can easily turn ugly, with the recipient often getting defensive and emotional.

So, let me share a simple strategy for giving negative feedback without creating drama. In other words, how to confidently discuss how you feel about someone's behavior or an issue without the recipient getting upset or you having to tippy-toe around it. This model is also great for delivering positive feedback.

The Four Step Feedback Approach (SBID)

I really like this approach, as it's simple and easy to both remember and deliver. You can prepare in advance and comfortably address the issue without incident.
First you need to prepare the recipient for the conversation, a simple "Hi Monica, can I talk to you for a few minutes?" is fine. You just need their undivided attention but please don't do a dramatic, big suspenseful build-up, just get them alone and focused.

S – Situation

Identify the specific situation that you want to give feedback on. Describe the specific situation in which the behavior occurred. For example, "This morning at the 11 a.m. team meeting" or "I would like to talk to you about your actions in Tuesday's team meeting" Avoid generalities, such as "one morning last week," as they can lead to confusion.

B – Behavior

For your feedback to be taken seriously, they need to clearly see your point of view. Just giving a sweeping statement or generalization won't cut it, you need to give them at least one specific example as evidence. Make sure you stay on point, avoid attacking the person's personality or beliefs. This will allow the person to listen without feeling like they are being insulted about who they are e.g. "In the team meeting on Tuesday, you were constantly interrupting me while I was telling the team about the monthly performance."

This will also help diffuse their objections and defensiveness, persons can argue opinions, but they can't argue facts.

I – Impact

At this point most people will be feeling under attack and defensive and it's now you are going to diffuse their reaction the most, explaining and describing the impact their behavior is having. If the effect was positive, using words like "pleased" or "impressed" help underscore the success of the behavior.

For example: "I was impressed when you addressed that problem without being asked."

If the effect of the person's behavior was negative and needs to stop, you can use words such as "concerned" or "worried."

For example, "I felt frustrated when you interrupted me because it diluted the importance of the message I was delivering."

Because you are describing exactly what happened and explaining your true feelings—not passing judgment—the person is more likely to listen and learn. Someone who has gotten into the habit of interrupting may not have realized the effect of his or her behavior. Conversely, the person who acted proactively may decide after positive feedback to continue to so.

D – Do

If the feedback was negative, they may be feeling a little confused, as sometimes they don't know how to change their behavior. Or they may be a little shocked as no one has been this honest with them before. They are now open to guidance on what to do next and even if they're not you will still need to set boundaries. At this point, you should clearly outline what you want them to do differently. Again, this highlights that you are focused on a single piece of behavior and are not attacking them as a person.

You can't just say "so stop acting the clown in meetings" as that is a personal attack. Instead try and give them an alternative behavior, at least this way you've given them every opportunity to change. So, for example "If you don't like my delivery style, that's ok. All I ask is that in team meetings, you let me speak until I am finished. After that I welcome you to constructively challenge the points raised, as I'm always open to feedback. Just let me get it all out before you do"

And that's it!

I recommend you take time to plan out and practice these conversations before any meetings. It does take practice to feel comfortable with the process, finding the right words, overcoming nerves etc. Don't worry if you don't get perfectly right, getting close will do. The key is you express how you honestly feel, without a personal attack and without candy-coating it to avoid confrontation.

Using a model like this is a great way to build confidence delivering uncomfortable messages, because you can just follow it without having to free-style or ad lib.

Adding the friend dynamic

While there's nothing wrong with employees having close personal relationships with one another, the dynamic between boss and employee is more complex and there's further messiness when you were friends before you became the boss!

When it comes to giving feedback to a friend, you're naturally going to be hypersensitive and without even thinking about it you will find yourself treating the person differently (divorcing yourself from the friendship in these scenarios comes with practice!) A good friend should respect the position even if they don't respect you and if you prep as per the model you'll be good! I would though add a couple of additional points from experience;

- Keep it totally professional and on topic – Don't be distracted and let your empathy keep you from addressing the situation. Conversely, you can use your friendship knowledge to your advantage by thinking about what it will be like to be in their situation. If things take a turn for the personal, remember your objective. If they get emotional, be sympathetic, but don't let it keep you from accomplishing your goal before ending the conversation.
- Give them an option – If you feel that you really can't be objective in the conversation or think it will be

awkward for your friend (especially if it's a disciplinary situation), offer options such as HR or another manager attending the meeting. Alternatively, let them make suggestions for ways to achieve change or to help them with their performance issue, show them that your dialogue can be positive.

*I add a note of caution – This move could be perceived as preferential treatment by other team members (and your Boss) so needs to be considered carefully as an option.

- When the conversation is over, and objective achieved, close it down quickly - Don't drag it on, it'll be uncomfortable for you both. Fight the urge to apologize to them or ask them how they are feeling. Allow them be in charge of their own next steps.

- Now is not the time to party - After your conversation, it's natural to want to bounce back to normal as though has happened between you, but fight this urge. Even it went perfectly well, your friend might need some time to digest your conversation and move on, hence giving them some space. Giving them the space, they need, will also show that you respect them as a person and co-worker as well preventing the preferential treatment scenario mentioned in the previous point.

- Don't stress about it - If your friendship is worth its salt, it will survive. A strong, mature, respectful relationship will handle a bump in the friendship road. You'll both emerge stronger than before and so will your friendship.

This woman can self-reflection questions;

- Using the Four Steps Model (SBID), think about a time you gave feedback (or an upcoming situation) and ask yourself;
- What are 3 key things that stand out to you as strengths - things you did well and should keep doing?
- What did you identify as your 3 biggest opportunities to improve? Any surprises?
- Is there anything that you want to consider starting to do?
- What about stopping or doing less of?

"Successful people use failures to sharpen their intuition by acknowledging mistakes for what they truly are - feedback."
Gordana Biernat

6. This Woman Can... navigate her relationship and her career.

Lena, worked as a Human Resource Director in an International company in Cayman. Aged 45, she was a divorcee with a 13-year-old daughter. Lena had worked for a number of big corporations for many years as a HR Manager having strategically, worked her way up the ladder with each move. Her partner Ian, ran his own small business and they had met three years, prior to her being employed in her current role.

Five months in to her role, Lena realized that the relationship between her and Ian felt strained. He was distant towards her, they were arguing more, and she didn't feel supported at home. During a heated conversation, Ian revealed that whilst he was happy that Lena was progressing in her career, he didn't feel motivated to match her efforts and in fact he felt a little intimidated by her success.

So, said Lena "What can I do to support him and keep our relationship strong?"

It's a common but often unspoken about scenario. No-one wants to admit or accept that their partner maybe jealous of, or intimidated by their success. Not trying to be sexist, but most times I see this happening in heterosexual relationships. After all, for years society has told us that the man should be the head of the household, be the main breadwinner, run things etc. and with this reversal their man pride is taking a little dent! Even if you are not competing in the same line of work, living with your success, can impact your partner's self-esteem and if you are more successful than them, you can probably expect there to be some tension in your relationship. Even when you're not in direct competition, a man's self-esteem tends to drop when his romantic partner is perceived to be more successful than he is.

So, you're striving to be the best person you can possibly be. You're taking steps to progressively improve your career, your life, you've got plans. But your partner? Not exactly. The challenge is addressing the source of tension with your partner without hurting or potentially alienating them so that you can both benefit from your achievements?

But first some real talk, when it comes to trying to change other people, that old saying is true: You can lead a horse to water, but you can't make it drink. Pressuring your partner to change doesn't work and could have a more negative than positive impact. However, if you are both flexible and willing to communicate, you can make the change and agree on a happy medium.

Communication is key – As women our self-esteem is closely linked to our feelings of adequacy in a relationship and we're less likely to feel threatened by direct competition but more likely to feel inadequate if our efforts aren't appreciated. Again, being careful not to stereotype, men tend to be far more competitive, they want their performance recognized more than the contribution they make on specific tasks. However, whilst everyone is different the common denominator is communication – so start talking.

First step? Take a walk in your partner's shoes! How do they really feel about your success? Is it jealousy and if so, why? Are you unknowingly flaunting your success over your partner? Have that honest conversation to identify where the tensions are. Don't be defensive, this is definitely a time you should be listening it's not a battle about which one of you is more accomplished. If you want to work this out, then both of you should be ready to listen without judgment and respect what the other person has to say.

Your way isn't the only way - No one likes being told what to do or being talked down to. Unsolicited advice often leads to reactance, a type of psychological resistance. If you really want to encourage behavior change, listen to your partner more than you speak. They have the same challenges you do with fear and self-doubt, so practice a little empathy and get to the bottom of what might be holding them back from making positive changes. Really, really try to avoid saying things like "You need to… (smoke/drink less, get a better career") or "Why don't you just… (Get organized, go back to school)." "How come you haven't…? (Submitted that application, followed up on that contact). Think about it, if someone had said the same disparaging questions to you in trying to have a supposedly constructive dialogue, how would you feel? Instead, replace advice giving with encouraging supportive questions, "How can I best support you right now? What would be helpful?" Once you're fully present and attentive to your partner's concerns, it creates an atmosphere of trust, laying the groundwork for collaborative problem-solving, allowing your partner open up and share their goals.

Recognize their efforts – Sense check yourself. Are you focusing solely on what's not going well? Are there activities taking place at home that are supporting you in your role? Focus on what's going well instead of criticizing what might seem wrong. Honest, specific praise is most effective for motivating and inspiring growth-mindset in others. Focusing on the good and expressing genuine love and support may spur your partner's internal motivation for change. In Lena's case, she recognized that she was projecting her own high standards on Ian. She'd committed to getting to the top of her career for herself and accepted that Ian's journey would be different and uniquely his.

Your success doesn't equal your partner's failure - It's important to understand that if you've surpassed your career goals, that doesn't mean that your partner has failed. It doesn't mean they've done something wrong. It just means that you're in different places when it comes to your work and you need to be as clear of what their aspirations are, as you are of yours. It's not meant to be a competition, but a partnership where you build each other up and support each other. It may take some time for them to get where you are – if that's their goal.

Are you living your relationship, or one built on expectations? - I referred to societal expectations/norms earlier, we all know times have changed especially with the increase of women at work. Your expectations in your relationship, should be based on the needs of your relationship not society, not your family or what your partner's friends' opinions are. Challenges begin when you start trying to live up to others expectations and they aren't met, they start judging you and you feel lacking.

In my own relationship, I saw a "role reversal" where my husband became a house husband and I became CEO. Did it make him feel any less of a man? Did I feel any less of a woman? No, because we'd had both agreed the dynamics of our relationship and understood if I was take on a demanding role our support structure would have to change. It was also a win-win situation as it allowed him to establish a business he could run from home whilst still being supportive. Point being, once both of you are content with your relationship and it works for you that's all that matters. The fact is, that a person's success is not defined by their gender, but their hard work and dedication.

Take your partner with you - Sharing your experiences will bring you closer together, foster love and a feeling of belonging. If you're concerned that you're growing apart, find ways you can involve your partner in your new habits or lifestyle. Lena and Ian started scheduling a monthly date night

– they had the rule of no phones during their date, so both were focused on each other. It was during one of their dates that Ian disclosed that he'd like to go back to school and Lena agreed to be his accountability partner and every time Ian completed a semester they rewarded themselves with a trip, so both benefitted from his growth.

Growth is natural in any relationship and it can be challenging when one partner evolves faster or differently from the other. But when you agree the stakes and lower and stress, making a change with your partner becomes much easier. If you want to help your partner change, support them in finding their own path. Let them know they can count on your support. Everyone needs someone in their corner when they go through the very vulnerable process of change.

Don't make it about the money, honey – You may unable to ignore the money! Money isn't the root of all evil, but if you have disparate incomes, it can be a devil! You may not talk about it, but you may display your new-found wealth, new clothes, make up, meals out etc., you want to enjoy the spoils of your labor. That's great, but your partner may feel a little out of sorts if they can't reciprocate – they want to make you happy too! They may feel you're being overly extravagant and that there are other priorities more important than the latest Coach bag, they're not going to say anything as you earned it, but they may be resentful. Arguing about money is one of the major factors in relationships and I tackle it in more depth in (Chapter 8. This Woman Can.....be the main breadwinner) but my advice is make sure you have the money conversations up front.

Watch the Power Dynamic - All relationships have a power dynamic and it's usually pretty evident who holds the reins. If you are more successful than your partner in a way that impacts the relationship, it is easy for you to assume that you should have the upper hand. For example, if you earn more than your partner or you have a bigger job title, you might fall into a pattern of controlling finances or making the financial decisions. The relationship power dynamic plays a role in conflict, persuasion, trust, and information sharing. When you think about your own relationship's power, it helps to remember that, for healthy relationships, power isn't a stable entity: It changes over time, across and within domains. What your power dynamic looks like now may be very different a few years down the line to come, as you tackle new challenges and adapt to new circumstances. So, check regularly to you know when you are pushing boundaries or it's out of sync for either of you. Make sure you are giving your significant other the space and support they need to grow, rather than simply maintaining the status quo. Just because you are unequal in some areas of your life does not stop you from being equal partners in your relationship.

Developing your careers—at any stage of a relationship is tough for both of you. While it would be nice if both of you could progress toward your career goals at the same pace, that's not realistic, and often unlikely. That means, at some point, one of you will be arguably more successful in your career than the other. If either of you are more successful in their career than the other during your relationship, it's normal to have feelings of being left behind, inadequacy and maybe even a little jealously. You should definitely acknowledge your feelings but don't let them take root and create bitterness between you and your partner. If you sense a change pull up your big girl pants and open the dialogue from a place of concern. Keep all the aforementioned points in mind to help you cope with your feelings and the situation in a healthy way - it's all about mindset.

This woman can self-reflection questions;

- What's the one thing bugging you in your relationship that you're not talking about?
- What's stopping you from addressing the situation?

- What do think will happen if you don't address it?
- What impact of addressing it, would you like to have?
- Who do you need to be have the conversation?
- What actions can you take to ensure you can have a constructive conversation?

"If your partner is angry with you, recognize that his anger is a misdirected plea for love. Your partner's simply upset because he feels something you said or did was a sign of not loving him enough."
Karen Salmansohn

7. This Woman Can... believe that she earned her seat at the table.

Georgina, was a 34-year-old highly successful team manager. She liked her job and was good at it, yet career progression wasn't happening for her. Everyone liked her, but didn't seem to see her as promotion material. An opportunity for promotion had arisen and she really wanted to take the next step in her career, but was afraid to approach the subject with her Boss because she was afraid that he would think negatively of her and her perceived lack of experience even though she regularly deputized for him in his absence. She knew based on the feedback from other managers, that on those occasions she did a really great job.

Georgina felt too embarrassed to talk about how she felt with anyone at work. She felt as if she were blowing her trumpet and wasn't at all comfortable owning her achievements. She loved where she worked but was thinking of leaving as a way to move forward, which put her in a real bind. She dreaded the thought of not fulfilling her potential as well as the thought of being ridiculed for her ambition. Even though she had demonstrated her abilities, she wasn't sure she could do it.

Georgina wanted help in deciding how to solve her "career" problem.

Georgina was suffering from impostor syndrome!

Impostor syndrome! It's much more common than you'd think and pretty much all of us have experienced it at some time or other in our lives. The thought of feeling like a fraud. Being unable to see or own our accomplishments, dismissing them as good luck, a product of perfect timing, or as a result of deceiving others into thinking that we're more intelligent and competent than they think we are.

Just so we're clear, let's define - Impostor syndrome. It's a psychological phenomenon that causes people to doubt their achievements and fear that others will expose them as fraudulent. The condition is non-discriminatory, it's believes in equal opportunity - it can affect anyone, regardless of their job, gender or social status but it mainly affects women! It's important to recognize and control it, as your sense of self-doubt helps you to determine a realistic assessment of your achievements, validity, competence and ability.

Over inflate your sense of doubt and it can be difficult to develop a realistic self-image. This is characterized by;

- Worry of not living up to the expectations of others – you fear that your colleagues and supervisors expect too much from you.

- Avoidance of extra responsibilities - you bury yourself in your routine work instead of taking on additional duties that can prove your abilities.

- Being stuck in the "impostor cycle" - success creates a continuous cycle of self-doubt. Every time you accomplish something, you worry that others will discover the "truth" about your abilities.

- Attributing success to outside factors - you deny your competency. You often feel that outside factors or chance are behind your successes. You might also believe that you need to work harder than everyone else.

- Becoming your own self-saboteur - your self-confidence maybe low and you have a fear of failure.
- Avoidance of being found out – you find yourself in a constant internal struggle between achieving success and avoidance of being "found out." This struggle prevents you from reaching your full potential.
- Lack of job dissatisfaction – you may feel unhappy in your job. You feel unchallenged, but a fear of failure or not being good enough stops you from seeking promotions or extra responsibilities.
- Denying your worth – you undervalue your skills and abilities as a result of being in denial of your worth, so you avoid asking for a raise because you don't believe you deserve more money for what you do.
- You over do (everything) – because of your intense fear of failure and the need to be the best you go overboard on tasks and goal-setting. You set yourself extremely challenging goals and suffer disappointment when you don't achieve them.

But all is not lost, you can overcome it, with some self-assessment and savvy strategies.

1. Acknowledge that impostor syndrome exists – once you accept it's a real thing, you'll be prepared to handle it if and when it appears.
2. Embrace positive feedback - when you receive it, embrace it with objectivity and internalize it. You did the work no-one else and when you deny the feedback, you're hurting that person's judgement.
3. Don't attribute your successes to luck – it was a result of your effort and your work.
4. Lose the denigrating language - don't talk about your abilities or successes using words like "just," "only," "simply," etc.

5. Log it - Keep a success journal, recording your successes and failures provides retrospective insight about them, and re-reading them makes you remember both of them equally.

6. Log it again – but this time don't just track your achievements, but also your progress. Women who suffer from imposter syndrome are mainly high achievers. We set high standards for ourselves, and if we see ourselves falling short of these standards it leads to us feeling like a failure and a fraud. Tracking your progress means you can set and celebrate small milestones on a regular basis. Experience 'winning' every time you surpass your personal milestones.

7. Kick Ms. Perfection into touch - Recognize that the perfect performer doesn't exist, accept that problems will occur eventually. Use them as lessons to move you forward.

8. Asking for help isn't a sign of weakness - it's okay to seek help from others and recognizing that you need help is actually a sign of strength.

9. Stop trying to prove that you're worthy - Do a great job – not because you have to prove yourself to your boss. Do it because you value great work. Do it because you have integrity. Do it because great work matters.

10. Realize that nobody knows what they're doing – I remember having a work issue and approaching my Boss to ask for his advice. "Look", he said, "I don't have all the answers. That's why I ask you, you might have a better solution given you're much closer to the issue". The big secret no one ever tells you is that nobody really knows what they're doing, we all started somewhere.

11. Pay less attention to the voice in your head - Do you ever wake up and genuinely think "I'm gorgeous, clever and capable. My body is absolutely perfect as it is. I can achieve anything I want." My guess is that's a

…no. Most of us wake up thinking the opposite and if we really sat and listened to our thoughts, we'd realize that it's mostly our inner mean girl praying on our concerns, fears and insecurities. The key to overcoming imposter syndrome is paying less attention to the voices in our head and pay attention to what's happening in the real world.

You are not an imposter. You are a fabulous individual who is on a continual, interminable learning curve; evolving, attaining and achieving – all on the road to glorious success.

This woman can self-reflection questions;

- Which of your successes are you not taking ownership of?
- Which of your beliefs about success are holding you back?
    - What do I need to do, to be, and to have in order to be successful?
    - Which beliefs are supporting you?
    - Which beliefs are holding you back?
    - What would be the effect of updating your beliefs?
    - How would things be different?

- Think of a time when performed well, what did you do particularly well?
    - Think about it, what do you notice?
    - What patterns, common factors are you seeing?
    - How you do to develop these strengths?
    - Look again, what's not on the list? What have you forgotten? What common themes do you see?

- How do you display these strengths in your day-to-day role?
- Which strengths could you use more?
- How could using these strengths benefit myself, my team and my organization?

"Sometimes I wake up at night and go, "Oh, damn! Here we go again! What were they thinking? They gave me this role; don't they know I'm faking it?"
Renée Zellweger

8. This Woman Can... be the main breadwinner.

Should women feel ashamed for earning more than their male partners?

What a provocative headline, one that really appeared in a newspaper article and one that really drove me mad!

Let me speak from experience here.

When I met my husband Derrick, whilst not a CEO (yet) I was successfully traversing the senior leadership ladder. I didn't tell him what I did for a job – I just told him that I worked in a call center (not that I ran a 250-seat operation). Whilst I was working my way up the ladder, Derrick already had a successful career in retail —and his salary reflected it. Eventually, my career grew. I got promotions and new jobs and the salary boosts that came with them. My salary surpassed Derrick's before we got married and continued to grow. His grew, too, but not at the same rate since persons in retail, unfortunately, make a fraction of what they deserve.

So, by default, I became the breadwinner and pretty much for our entire relationship I've earned more. Whilst we never made a big deal about it, I was cognizant of the salary differences and we agreed to contribute to the family budget proportionately to our earnings – sometimes he chipped in a little more than me on things like nights out and the car.

Back then our arrangement would have been the exception, but female breadwinners are now becoming the norm and when a woman makes more money than her partner, the income imbalance can affect the relationship. I hear it all the time coaching successful women, who feel that earning more than their partner will put a strain on their personal relationship and to be honest I feel this more a reflection of the male ego (I haven't come across it in same sex relationships). It can become such a bone of contention that it warrants its own discussion point!

Questions regarding budget management, childcare, and household responsibilities can also be grounds for contention and a major source of stress, so in essence whilst there can be some logistical challenges, the real issue isn't about money but other external factors;

Societal Pressure – Despite the growth of female breadwinners, people still look sideways at couples where the woman has the higher-powered job and the man either has a lower-paying one or stays at home. It's a strange dynamic, most times they admire and applaud the woman on being successful – (well done you) and if you're a single mother that admiration goes up a few more notches as that supports their rationale as to why you're the breadwinner. But woe betide if you're part of a couple, family, friends and co-workers may say or imply that the woman in this relationship is being taken advantage of. Smacks of double standards as no one questions when the woman in the relationship earns less or stays at home - that's a good thing and she's a great mom doing wonderful things for her family!

Internal Feelings – If you and/or your partner were raised as part of a "man brings home the bacon and mom stays at home" family, one of you might struggle with the female breadwinner dynamic. We internalize the way we were raised as that was the "right way" and going against conflicts with how we feel. Women might feel resentment and men may feel inadequate.

Stress – Being the breadwinner brings is its own kind of stressful. We may not want to feel solely responsible for all of the family's financial needs. Maybe we want to be at home raising the kids, maybe we want to work on our entrepreneurial pursuits but can't since all the income and the insurance is attached to your job. What if you lose your job, become ill, what if……? I'm sure men experience the same level of stress about all the things that could go wrong.

Resentment – Along with stress can come resentment - it can be hard to see friends/colleagues/family members who "get to", work a less stressful job, take their kids to school, stay at home have fun with the kids when they're on holiday or launch their own business funded by their partner's income and wishing you were in their shoes.

As always, communication is the key and both of you need to agree what works for you both;

1. **Define your own rules** – Don't worry about society thinks, it's your relationship and you need to do what results in an effective partnership for you both. Take a pragmatic approach and let go of traditional ideals by writing your own rules.

2. **Agree the trade-offs** – To lessen the psychological impact, identify the trade-offs you both need to make to maintain your circumstances. Whether it's you take turns on the school run or your partner feeling they lack the autonomy they once had, this is your combined reality.

3. **Managing the budget** – Can't escape the money, but this is often more emotional than logical, so we avoid the conversation. But to make your relationship work it's essential you figure out a financial structure that works for your specific demands – one that's fair for both of you. It needs to be functional, it might mean joint or separate finances but it's one you both agree

on. Calculate your expenses and divide them according to your interests and strengths. Make sure you plan for unexpected eventualities, invest for your kids' higher education, holidays, your own retirement too, nothing is out of bounds.

4. **Discuss your financial goals** – You may earn more and so believe it's your money to spend how you please. It is, but if you're partner is saving for an undisclosed goal such as a holiday or a home improvement and sees you with the newest handbag there's bound to be a little tension, so make sure you're both clear on your financial priorities.

5. **Keep your partner's feelings in mind** – It's not just about balancing the financial side of your relationship, you need to address the emotional one too. To keep from feeling resentful you need to be open, honest and receptive about each other's feelings. This includes acknowledging the psychological impact when your partner isn't able to act as provider, it shouldn't be ignored.

6. **Don't use money as a form of power** – Earning more can make you feel like you have the upper hand when it comes to decisions. Wrong! If you want your relationship to survive when you make more, don't use money as a form of power when it comes to decisions, purchases, etc. Remember, you are a team and your partner doesn't want it held over their head that you make more — no score keeping of the financial imbalance, or inequities in the household. If there are issues, work to resolve them together.

7. **Your home** – it might seem like a strange point to raise here but when you're feeling stressed about being the sole/main provider then you'll find some way to vent your stress and often that can be the time you become House Proud Hattie and find everything wrong at home! Real talk, your partner will never be as concerned with the state of your home as you are.

Adapt by establishing defined roles and, if your kids are old enough, include them in the discussions surrounding tasks so that everyone's on the same page. It might be difficult, but you may need to lower (sharp intake of breath!) your expectations, and even turn a blind eye sometimes, to maintain a happy home!

8. **Your partnership** - If you have kids in the mix, flexibility and compromise are key to assuming parenting roles that draw on both of your strengths and skills.

9. **It's your business and no-one else's** – Friends, family, the world will always have an opinion and that might be criticism of your arrangement and what they regard as 'alternative' choices. What works for you isn't their concern and needs no explanation. Once you have each other's back during the hard times – you're on the same team.

We started off talking about money, but as you can see it's not always about the money honey! How you split financial responsibilities is entirely up to you and different couples will handle their finances in different ways. The key is to have the discussion and agree to arrange monies in a way that allows both partners to have independence and a fair share of financial responsibility, regardless of your respective career success.

This woman can self-reflection questions;

- What impact does money have on your relationship?
- How often do you discuss money matters with your partner?

"If you love somebody, you love them. My parents had a 25-year age gap between them and my mum was the breadwinner, my dad the house husband. I'm a strong believer that a good relationship can work, whatever the situation."
Katherine Jenkins

9. This Woman Can... confidently navigate the Board Room!

Nicola had just been appointed CEO having worked her way through the ranks to attain her position. Being part of a larger group, she was required to present her business performance at a monthly meeting with the predominantly male Board of Directors. Although she had attended a couple of previous meetings as part of the mentorship she'd received from her former Boss, she had never delivered a Board presentation. To compound the situation, her business performance that month had been poor, and she'd heard nerve racking anecdotes of how previous CEO's who delivered poor performances had been verbally abused and even thrown out of meetings. She was anxious to deliver a good presentation and leave a great impression.

Her coaching focus - "How do I navigate the complexities of the Board room, get my message across and leave them wanting more?"

I'm not going to butter it up or paint a pretty picture – the boardroom can be the worst place to deliver a presentation (personally I'd rather have stood up in front of a thousand strangers than have delivered my first Board presentation). But if you are in senior leadership or aspire to be, it would be unusual for you at some point not to present in the boardroom (or your business' equivalent). It can be an arduous, stress inducing process, but the following techniques can help you to be more successful when it's your turn to shine in the boardroom.

Before the meeting

Understand the Boardroom culture – No matter what industry, the objective of every Board is usually the same – it's a place of reckoning. It is where senior management and executives go to flog the last bad period of results and beat up those accountable – which could be you! Hence just entering the boardroom conjures up images of a gladiator ring - with you on the defensive, armed with your presentation and data facing the offensive Board Directors poised to give you the thumbs down if they don't like what they hear. The boardroom is not the place to reveal new ideas – it is a place to torture suspected sinners, punish under-performers and destroy visionaries. Never deliver new ideas in your boardroom presentation. You could get lucky, your Board might be civilized, but the objective is still the same.

Find yourself a Board room mentor – Find and talk to a colleague who has attended meetings and can help you disseminate fact from fiction. We all know that anecdotal stories of boardroom battles can be embellished and sensationalized – so get as factual as possible. Before the meeting, review your presentation with your mentor, work with to identify any performance issues that maybe honed in on. Work with them to draft corrective actions – you may not use them, but the powers that be like to you know you have thought of solutions even if they don't agree with them.

Know who are key players - This maybe the first and only time you come face to face with your Board members and whilst you don't know them personally, it helps to understand their main focuses. Know who they are, and their pet likes and dislikes. Even though a Board acts as one body in the interests of the organization, there is still a hierarchy

Beware of any topical issues – Are there any issues that have been identified from previous meetings, insider jokes or unwritten rules? Difficult to ascertain prior to a meeting but just be aware that curveballs can be thrown that could put off your presentation.

Proofread your presentation – If you're like me, then there's nothing worse to throw you off your presentation than spotting grammar slips and typos plus they impact your communication credibility with the Board. Aside from being an eloquent presenter, you also need to show that you're a capable writer. Take the time to double-check your slides for any errors. Fact check any key points you're trying to make and to be extra sure, ask someone else to proofread your content.

Prep the morning before your presentation - If there is anything you need you still have time to get it. Have a backup copy of your presentation both digital and print. Decide what you'll wear – nothing worse in finding out your lucky bra/dress/pants needs cleaning! Don't leave anything to chance.

Familiarize yourself with the venue - Can you do a reconnaissance session of the presentation location? Get a feel for the size of the room, the seating layout, and the acoustics? Not always possible but you can never have too much information.

Boardroom etiquette – Be clear about the expectations of you in the Boardroom. What's the dress code? How soon should you arrive prior to the meeting? Is there a pre-meeting with your Boss before you present? Will you present alone or have support? Do you present and solicit questions at the end or will questions be thrown at you during your presentation. These all may seem minor but can make or break your confidence.

Self-Preparation

What's your style? - Unsurprisingly, Boards tend to be male dominated and will be so until the foreseeable future, so your challenge will be identifying and developing your Board presentation style. How do you remain true to who you are and what got you to this point without compromising your authenticity? Hearing of the combative nature of the Boardroom there may be a tendency to adopt a masculine delivery style – after all we've had very few role models to emulate and if you look closely at those who did make it, they've adopted some masculine tendencies. There's really no right answer to what your style is, other than make it one you are you comfortable with in an already stressful situation. You got to this point because you had something about you and I would say that the most effective leaders stay true to themselves at all times. So, trust yourself, your instinct, your inner strength – you can do this.

Clarify the impact you want to have in the boardroom - Once you understand who you are, be clear in your mind about exactly what you want to achieve. Focus on developing your professional presence, with physical, vocal and practical exercises. Whose delivery style do you like? Is it a style you can adapt to suit you? Women naturally tend to have better emotional intelligence i.e. the ability to identify and manage both your own and other emotions and apply them to tasks like thinking and problem solving; so, use it to your advantage. Be aware of emotional cues, show empathy, support and your integrity where and whenever possible. Being confident and clear in your own mind about what you want to achieve will help with your natural and authentic delivery style.

Impress and establish credibility - As there have been so few women at the Board level that means there are few comparative historical role models. Great, this means you can set the standard of what good looks like. You will demonstrate business credibility via your presentation content, but personal credibility will be delivered by you. So, whilst they can't see your nerves churning on your insides, they can see your external behavior. This will be used to decide your credibility. Practice the use of some of the techniques referred to below you can easily establish credibility with your audience.

- **Body Language/Non-Verbal** - First impressions count, and your impact starts before to speak and will influence their expectations! Walk into the room or on stage in a relaxed, calm way, with a soft smile and make eye contact with your audience as you walk to the podium or the spot where you are going to start speaking.

- **Maintain eye contact** - truthfulness and confidence is acquainted with the ability to make and hold eye contact. Too little eye contact will make you look untrustworthy. Too much will make you look crazy and aggressive. Make sure you capture every by mentally diving the room into zone and scan each one for 2-3 seconds per person.

- **Stand confidently** - upright with feet hip width apart and toes turned out very slightly. This will make you look and sound a more confident and credible speaker. (Quick note – make sure the shoes you're wearing are comfortable – not too high or squeezing your bunions, this is not the time for fashion choices!)

- **Move with purpose** – no pacing, fidgeting, rocking or swaying. Harness all these anxiety distractions. This will help you look more confident, energetic and engaging when you speak.

- **Exit confidently too** – it can be easy to just fall into a relaxed pose, let out a huge sigh and rush off as if you cannot wait to get away. This too creates an impression of nervousness and will undermine all the good work you did.

- **Every word counts** – the way you speak can also have an impact on the way the Board perceives your authority and presentation! So consciously slow down when you speak. Get comfortable pausing as it will not only gives you more time to think, but again more credibility and authority.

During the meeting

Know your numbers – Board meetings are often focused on performance, so you need to know your core KPI's and their levers (what has/will impact their performance). If you don't know the answer, then please, please don't make it up – you will be found out! State you're unclear of the answer but will clarify at the end and update the Board accordingly.

Be upfront – If you know your performance isn't brilliant or there's something adverse in what you have to deliver, don't skirt over it or hide it. Be upfront about the issue – highlight the problem but deliver/suggest solutions/remedies. Demonstrate that you're in control of your business but again do not bullshit the board – they've been there and done that. They're hold a board position because of their knowledge and you don't play a player!

Stay focused on your SIMPLE presentation – In my experience, the board just doesn't have time for detail. You're the only one that needs to know the excruciating detail, the board doesn't have time for all that. They would have been supplied will all the background information they need and will be judging and debating proposals based on big ideas, not details. You probably have no longer than 15 minutes to present and they have the same time to decide. Focus on the specific details you want to get across not because you want to prove how savvy you are.

Read the room – This is just another meeting on a more intense scale – same as you would in any meeting pick up on the body language signals – nods or frowns. Are you engaging the audience? Are notes being made at key points in your presentation?

Don't over talk – if you have nothing tangible to add keep your mouth shut. Do not embellish your presentation unless you've been asked to provide additional information. You may find yourself going into uncharted territory that you have not prepared for. If a Board member speaks, do not interrupt let them finish and then ask for clarity on any points not understood or paraphrase to ensure you've picked up the main points prior to answering.

Remember, it's not personal – The Board's interest is in the business performance and is very rarely about you, so if it feels you're fighting for your life, their sole interest is ensuring that the business' needs are being met and that they have a capable person at the helm.

After the meeting

Seek feedback and reflect – If possible seek feedback on your performance – not just from the Directors (if you're close enough) or your Boss, but from the independent parties. Often, there's someone in the room taking the minutes – a PA or Secretary – they pretty much attend every meeting and can provide you with objective feedback. They're also great future allies and a source of information – keep them on your side.

Follow up – Were there any actions given? If so what were they yours and what were the deadlines? Make sure you follow through on them. If you didn't capture all or unsure of what they were– remember the PA or secretary allies? This is where they can step in.

Remain tight lipped (Snitches get stitches) – Confidentiality is paramount – you may share or hear business sensitive information which if divulged to the wrong person could impact negatively on your organization. So, what is said in the Boardroom, stays in the Boardroom.

Breathe – Well done, it's over and you survived until next time so be kind to yourself. If this was your first Board you'd have been an absolute bundle of nerves and probably incredibly tense – so take a breath, congratulate yourself you survived your first Board room encounter – it's all uphill from here.

This woman can self-reflection questions;

- Who could you approach to be your Boardroom mentor?
- What do you know about your Board members and where could you source additional information?
- What is the presentation style and format of your organization's Board?
- On a scale of 1-10 (10 being the highest), if you were asked to deliver to your Board next week, how prepared would you be? If less than 7, what would make you a 9 or 10?

"We need women who are at the head of a boardroom, like at the head of the White House, at the head of kind of major scientific enterprises so that little girls everywhere can then think, you know what? I can do that, I want to do that, I will do that."
Chelsea Clinton

10. This Woman Can... say no, without damaging her career!

In my previous corporate life, I was asked to attend an overseas business trip that was right in the middle of a personal vacation that included my family and a very expensive hotel. Being a seasoned corporate vet, I said no on this occasion due to the importance of the vacation and outlined where on other occasions I've actually been more amenable and accommodated such last-minute requests. However, I was pretty confident and resolute in my decision (and maybe a little pissed off) so was able to take a firm stance, but I know some of you may not be so confident.

Maybe there's times you've been asked to work over or change your day off, been given last minute requests to make changes to a piece of work or you just generally don't want to do what's been asked of you. As women we have many demands/situations where our time and attention is demanded, often leaving very little time for own sanity and precious me time. As I'm writing this I'm realizing that there are numerous areas where you may want to say no but just haven't felt confident to do so, such as your Boss, Colleagues, Partner/Husband, Children and whilst there maybe similarities in some of the skills needed to say the 'No" there is no one size fits all, cookie cutter method. So, for this chapter I'm going to focus on how to say no to your Boss.

So, what would could you do to make saying NO a little more comfortable?

First try and understand why you find it hard to say no?

- Is it fear of rejection – you don't want to disappoint someone, make them angry, hurt their feelings, or appear unkind or rude? We all want to be liked and feel that we're not letting anybody down, but does that have to be at the expense of how we feel?
- Are you trying to impress at work? A demanding boss/colleague/people pleasing there plenty of scenarios here and you get the usual per pieces of advice to avoiding requests such as put your phone on silent, especially when not to open email. etc., but that option is often short lived, and they'll keep asking you.

Don't fear the No!

- It may seem like a powerfully intimidating two letter word. But for such a tiny word, "no" is intensely liberating. When you decide, "this does not warrant my immediate attention, or this is counterproductive we're not doing this" you'll feel a hell of a lot better.
- This may sound like an anomaly but saying No starts with effective communication. People will eventually respect you for disagreeing with them. Saying "no" doesn't make you a bad person. It's quite the opposite. It shows you have a vision, a plan, and an opinion. By clearly articulating your needs, challenges, or deadlines you begin to eliminate distractions. In turn, you stop feeling inclined to people please because you have defined a game-plan.

What happens if you keep saying yes?

Whilst you think constantly saying yes to everything to your Boss asks you to do, will make you look like a great employee or the best team player, it can lead to negative repercussions such as you;

- Develop a reputation for poor work as you took much on and can't meet the deadline.
- End up doing other people's work for them instead of properly delegating.
- Find yourself working extra hours so you can't focus on your personal goals
- Sacrifice sleep, exercise, and time with people you enjoy
- Develop a reputation for being approachable but not reliable
- Have people nagging you about when they will get things done
- Start feeling overwhelmed, inadequate, guilty, frustrated, and resentful

It's all good doing a job and displaying a willingness to serve, acting like a team player etc., all are great qualities. But when you allow every request to divert your attention from your most important activities of the day, nobody wins. So, when you decide enough is enough, it's how you respond and say that first no that matters!

Should I Say No to The Boss?

If you're presented with a "should I say No to my Boss" situation at work, ask yourself a few questions

- Am I already working on several important assignments that will leave me no time for this one?
- Can I delegate some of my other work to subordinates or colleagues to enable me to take on this assignment?

- Can I pause some of my other assignments while I work on this one?
- Will taking on this assignment cause me to neglect or lessen my attention to another important one?
- Do I have, or can I quickly acquire the skills necessary to complete this assignment?
- Am I the only person in the business who has the skills to complete this assignment?

Conversely, whilst it may seem like a good idea at the time, there are some great reasons not to turn down your Boss' request – especially in these scenarios;

- **You think the task is too difficult** - If you have the skills to do the job, but feel it will take more effort than you're willing to make, turning it down will reflect poorly on you.
- **It's not part of my job description** – I've not come across a job description that could define a role 100%. You should be willing to go outside of your job description as long as you can do the work.
- **I'm in the middle of planning my birthday party/vacation/wedding/baby shower or insert any other personal even**t – Don't be naïve, a personal event should never take precedence over anything that is part of your job, you're not getting paid for that.
- **You feel you're being taken advantage of** - Unfortunately, not everyone can have the world's best boss title and if you happen to work for a bad one, then chances are they'll try to take advantage of you at every opportunity. So, if you find yourself working late every night or constantly running personal errands for your boss (which have nothing to do with your work), then now's a good time to start putting your foot down or look for a new job!

- **You're concerned that your values will be compromised** - Again, not an easy one but if what you're being asked to do goes against your personal values and makes you feel uncomfortable doing it, then say something up. If you're not enthused by what you're being asked to do, then you won't produce your best work. Hopefully, your boss will appreciate your honesty. If what you're being asked to do is illegal or unethical, say 'no' immediately!
- **You don't feel like doing it** - Remember, there's always someone knocking at the door waiting for your job aka your boss won't think twice about hiring someone else who actually wants to do what they're being asked to do.
- **You're new** - The truth is that if you're within the first six months of a new job, waiting to pass probation and know you want to be made permanent in the role, you need to be more of a 'yes' woman (or man) if you want to prove your worth as a hardworking motivated team member.

So How Do I say NO?

Now that you know when it's ok and not ok to say 'no' to El Hefe we'll tackle how you utter the word:

- Make sure that you've fully considered and evaluated the validity of the reasons you're saying 'no' in the first place.
- If you're still unsure, try and buy yourself some time to figure out whether you can or can't honor the request. Say something like: 'Can I have a couple of hours to think this through and see where it fits alongside my other priorities?'

- Phrase how you say no, don't just come out with a hard NO. Cushion what you're about to say. Instead of saying 'No, I don't have time for that' or 'No, that's not my job', take a more tactful approach to explaining your reason. Something like 'I would be love to work on that project, but I've got two deadlines coming up, and I don't think I would be able to work on it this week'.

- Sometimes you are asked to do something, and you would really like to get involved with but don't have the time. When this happens, suggest or ask how you can contribute in a way that works for you in the time you want to commit. This will keep you involved but on your terms.

- No double talk, be clear on what you're trying to say. It's important that you explain your reasons (whatever they may be) as clearly and as straightforward as possible to avoid any possible misunderstandings. For instance, saying something as ambiguous as 'I can't do that now' can be taken to mean 'I'll be able to do it in half an hour'.

- Don't be the problem, become the solution and suggest an alternative. Your Boss will love that you've thought about the challenge and can offer solutions to their problems. This can be a great opportunity to shine and showing that you care about the business. Even though you can't complete the task yourself, offering an alternative will help you stay in your boss's good books.

- For goodness sake don't lie, be honest and true about your reasons, because trust me a good Boss will discover the truth later down the road if you lie to them. Which will only reflect badly on you and result in a loss of trust.

- Lastly, don't be rude: There really is no need to be mean or resentful, no matter how much you feel put out. So that means no sighing, no chupsing (for my fellow Caribbean's), no lip curling, no scowling, no eye rolling, no stropiness and definitely don't say in a whiney voice "It's not my turn!" Check your tone, body language and overall response, try to be polite about your rejection. Find the perfect balance of control and affability.

If you've developed a reputation for always being able to meet your Boss' requests, you may have a few people who don't like your new approach. But keep practicing better responses, you'll end up making more people happy – including yourself.

This woman can self-reflection questions;

- How do you feel when you have to say No to someone in authority?
- What do you think makes you have these feelings?
- What makes you feel like you have to say yes to requests, you really want to say no to?
- What could you say instead of No?

> **"I have had to learn about saying no."**
> **Jaclyn Smith**

11. This Woman Can... not take things personally.

Eleanor had been experiencing a significant amount of change at work. There had been a major reorganization which had impacted her role, along with seeing a number of her colleagues being laid off and her responsibilities increase in some areas but decrease in others. Her manager was situated in another country and she relied on weekly virtual meetings (which sometimes got cancelled last minute due to her Manager having to attend with more important issues). This annoyed Eleanor as, even though her Boss kept reassuring her that her job was safe, it was really the only time she got to air her concerns or seek clarity of what was expected of her in the new restructure. With minimal direct contact from her manager she just continued to focus on what she thought her role now entailed. But she was still unsettled and was disconcerted as she had overheard other team members talk about changes in other departments and someone laughing about people who thought their jobs were safe. Eleanor was convinced that her manager wasn't sharing information with her and that her job was on the line.

"I'm sure she's just biding her time to tell me my job is going and that everyone is just laughing at me" How can focus on my job and not take things personally?"

In uncertain times, this kind of thinking can be hard to escape, and it can be especially troublesome when you can't rid yourself of the memories from previous unpleasant work environments. Uncertainty breeds vulnerability even after you've moved on. You can't quite shake the idea that things aren't that different or improved so you constantly question the motives of your colleagues.

If your natural tendency is to worry or you always feel anxious, your paranoia is likely to be even worse. For instance, whilst at a conference, I overheard a comment, that whilst not directed at me I took personally. What the comment was, was neither here nor there but think of all the times you've taken random comments or persons actions to heart because you felt personally impacted – you thought someone looked at you "funny" or gave you side eye, a job you didn't get, the loan that got rejected! You logically tell yourself it's can't be personal because you don't know the people involved for them to give you that look, you're a random application to that employer! It's not personal but it feels very personal!

Low self-esteem is can make it hard for you to accept the pleasant nature of your current workplace at face value. When suspicion, fear, and persistent worst-case scenario thinking threaten to negatively impact the quality of your work life, your only response must be to ditch the paranoia once and for all.

To get along in life, careers, relationships, we have to learn not to take things personally, take things in our stride, let things roll off our backs rather than letting them pierce our heart, the happier and more resilient we'll be. So how do you get there?

Be Your Confident Self - The more inner confidence you have and the value of your work, the less likely you are to take umbrage if someone criticizes what you've done, you or your work. Confidence acts as a buffer between you and the comments and actions of other people. The more confident you are, the thicker that buffer is. This kind of confidence is difficult to develop and can take time, but remember that our brains are wired to focus on the negative so you're probably harder on yourself than you deserve. Take some time to focus on your own accomplishments – where are you versus 1 year, 5 years, 10 years ago. What's changed, how far have you moved forward? Talk to someone who likes an, respects you, and let them remind you of how awesome you are. Understanding your own value is your best defense when someone makes you feel small.

Recognize your own triggers - All of us have things that push our buttons and set off reactions that may be out of proportion to reality. Make the effort to be aware of those triggers and how you react to them. I tend to hate comments about single parents and the associated statistics – the generalization that single moms can't amount to much makes me mad! Knowing I have this trigger doesn't stop me from having those feelings, but I can sometimes catch myself and say, "Wait a minute – you know that's not true as you know loads of successful single parents including myself." That gives me a chance to put things into perspective.

We all have sensitivities but being aware of these tender spots and how you may tend to over-react when they come up in conversation is the goal. Don't allow yourself to get sucked into feeling bad when these topics are brought up.

Be logical - Stop! Look at the situation calmly and rationally, you will see that the slight or insult that upset you wasn't really such a big deal, or has an easy explanation.

Question Your Beliefs - We're often not affected by people's actions but by our interpretation of their actions. In turn, our interpretations are formed by our beliefs. For instance, you walk into a room and say good morning/good day as is customary and a woman doesn't acknowledge you. Your beliefs kick into overdrive and sound something like this;

If I greet someone, they have to greet me back.

If they don't return my greeting, they're being disrespectful.

If they're disrespectful, it's because they think that I'm not worthy of respect.

If people think I'm not worthy of respect, then they think I'm worthless.

If people think I'm worthless, then maybe I am.

You can see how that line of thought would lead to us feeling bad.

I, on the other hand, don't get upset if people don't greet me when I greet them, because my beliefs are the following:

I greet people when I walk into a room, because I think it's the polite thing to do, but not everyone has the same manners.

If they don't greet me back it's not about me, but about them. There could be a load of explanations why they didn't return my greeting: they didn't hear me; they don't speak English; they're having a bad day; or they simply think it's best not to talk to people they don't know.

So, because of my beliefs I know it's not about me - If you want to stop taking things personally, question your own beliefs.

Stop worrying so much about what other people think of you - The only reason why you would take something someone says about you personally is if the approval of the person you're interacting with is important to you. Recognize the following:

- You've been conditioned since birth (read brainwashed) – into thinking that you have to belong and be accepted by others.
- The truth is, not everyone has to like and accept you.

- You don't have mind meld powers and can't control what others think of you. Even if you follow all of the "rules" and do everything "right", how others respond to you is outside of your circle of influence.
- If you accept yourself, and act in the way that you think is right, you'll attract people who will accept you for who you are. That is, people around whom you don't have to worry about what they're thinking of you, because you know they love you.

Recognize the "Spotlight Effect" - Most times when we feel that we're been judged or criticized by someone else, it's all in our heads. We're acutely aware of our flaws, weaknesses, and insecurities and so magnify them, usually all out of proportion.

For the most part other people are totally unaware of your perceived flaws. Therefore, you may think that you picked up on some criticism from a colleague, when the reality is that they weren't talking about you at all.

Think about this: without a doubt there have been times in the past when you've taken something personally, when what was said wasn't even about you. Keep that in mind the next time you're tempted to take something personally.

Think: "Girl/Boy bye Delete" - The absolute worst place for misconstruing comments is social media. How many times have you posted something and received a disparaging comment from some random individual, who doesn't even know you? Or seen a friend's post that has hundreds of comments because he/she inadvertently took offence and engaged in comment warfare? These keyboard warriors comments really aren't worth your time, they don't know you, the circumstance or situation, so don't take them seriously. Don't dwell on them, don't give them the power to make you feel bad about yourself – just ignore and move on to something actually worth your time and attention.

The next time someone posts something negative about you out of the blue, just think: "Girl/Boy bye Delete"

You only have so much time and energy, right? Life's far too short to give others the power to make your life miserable? Being over sensitive can feel like you are always getting hurt, but you don't have to suffer. There are things you can do to be less vulnerable as suggested but the biggest thing is to have confidence in who you are.

This woman can self-reflection questions;

- What's the one situation that making you feel anxious/nervous/paranoid right now?
- What proof do you have that the facts surrounding the situation are true?
- Who could you talk to verify?

"Try not to take things personally. What people say about you is a reflection of them, not you."
Anon.

12. This Woman Can... manage feeling overwhelmed.

Natalie and I had been working together for a number of months, she had successfully navigated the office politics and nepotism to land her dream job of project manager and quite rightly, she was pleased of her career progress. However, at our usual session I could see she wasn't her usually bubbly self – her eyes were dark, and she didn't look her usually immaculate self. "I'm exhausted, I volunteered to support another team which comes with some additional workload. But, I'm still balancing 4-5 of my own projects, I'm feeling a little out of my depth. I really don't want to turn away the work, especially since it could be repeat clients or referrals. But it just so much, I don't know how to manage, and I don't want to let my team down. I just so feel overwhelmed."

Natalie had worked hard to achieve her first leadership position and obviously wanted to make the most of it – she still had plans to go higher in the organization and was not prepared to fall at her first hurdle.

It is not at all uncommon to feel overwhelmed at some point in your life. A variety of life experiences may bring on such feelings. Ranging from multiple significant life issues, challenges or transitions occurring in rapid order; a lack of coping resources, such as: supportive, caring friends, families or communities; rewarding involvements outside of work life; appropriate self-care or stress management skills; or, sometimes, a lack of a sense of overarching meaning or purpose in one's life.

There's no one reason that causes overwhelm, unfortunately the possibilities are endless. It varies by individual, so what feels like overwhelm to you can feel like a walk in the park to others. For working women this can be particularly challenging with demands appearing to come from all fronts.

- At work, spans of control have broadened and at the same time if you're a leader you're expected to accomplish more with fewer resources.
- At home, we have family demands and we wonder how we can possibly do everything we're supposed to do and still have some kind of a personal life.

To summarize it can impact anybody and be impacted by anything!

Imagine, the kids are fighting, your partner's vex because you forgot an important meeting, you missed breakfast, your boss moved your deadline to the end of the day and damn you didn't have time to do your hair (again!). Technology was supposed to free us up and enable us to work less and pay more attention to the most important things in our lives. Unfortunately, those predictions were dead wrong. We may not be getting paid for working more hours than we were twenty years ago, but given smartphones, email and colleagues in a variety of time zones, many of us seem to be spending a lot more time in work-related activities than ever before.

So, what do you do when it all feels like too much? When you start to feel overwhelmed?
This is not about having all, it's about finding the strategies that work best for you:

1. **Ask yourself, am I being paid to do this?** - I know I was guilty of this – spending far too much time doing things that other people can and should be doing. Sometimes it's because it's a task we like doing it; it's

comfortable, it's fun, it's a distraction but in all honesty, it should now be someone else's job. Sometimes we don't trust others to do it the way we want it done - but if we keep doing it ourselves, it will create a blockage and hold up activities. I know it's seems easier at times but it's time to kick the habit and it hand off, doing so will reduce your workload and allow you to focus on where you need to be. Over the next few days, before you tackle a task, ask yourself: Is this a task I should be doing? Is there anyone else who can do this? If the answer to the first question is no but the second question is yes - delegate!

2. **Are you meeting for meetings sake?** – We've all been there, summoned to a meeting only to wonder why am I here, this could have been an email! How much time do we spend in meetings? Research indicates that if you're a middle manager, it's likely about 35% of your time, and if you're in senior management, it can be a whopping 50% and that's not counting the 4 hours per week spent preparing for the meeting. If you're a leader it's your responsibility as a leader, both to yourself and to those you lead, to make meetings as worthwhile as possible. Before you start the meeting: make sure that everyone in a meeting knows "STOO" –Subject, Time, Owner, Objective. That is,

Subject - What are we talking about?

Time - How long are we going to spend on it?

Owner - Who actually needs to be in the meeting – who's responsible for moving it forward?

Objective - Most importantly - why are we having the meeting?

If you get into the habit of clarifying these points or asking others to clarify it for their own meetings, everyone's time will be much better spent.

3. **Getting sucked into the vortex** – aka Time Stealers. These are activities we get sucked into, (sometimes) self-generated tasks and conversations that are simply unproductive. We all know how easily it can happen – in my previous CEO life I can recall some mornings when I'd take an hour to get to my desk because I'd be stopped on my journey from car to desk by customers, vendors and employees. Or taking a rejuvenation break and having had an impromptu meeting on the way. Now there's no problem having a light-hearted, casual conversation with a colleague, or getting outside for a few minutes fresh air, they all have their place. Just be mindful of the time stolen by these activities and make sure that when you are engaged in time stealing activities, they actually support your mental, physical and emotional wellbeing.

4. **Is it necessary?** - Numerous times, we do things - both professionally and personally - because we assume "we have to," or "we've always done that." I worked in an environment where I was constantly being asked to produce reports. These weren't simple reports they were the type you had to pull together from numerous sources so incredibly time consuming when your back was already against the wall. I then noticed that I was constantly being asked for information that was contained in the report that I had already painstakingly pulled together. Suspecting that no one actually read said report, I stopped submitting. Lo and behold, no one chased me for it – I was reporting for reporting's sake! So, think about the things you do regularly that feel like a waste of time. Is it adding value given the time spent? If you stopped doing them altogether, what would be the outcome? Is there an easier way of completing the task? In the case of my reporting, it was simply that it was easier for the recipient to make

me do the work as he could have easily ran the reports himself.

5. **Find time to breathe** - This may seem entirely counter-intuitive when you're super busy, but I've seen it work wonders for myself and others. No matter how up against it you are, take some time – even 20 minutes out of the day – to step back and assess your life and work from a distance, it will help you use the rest of your time much more effectively. I actually scheduled lunchbreaks in my diary and marked them as private, so no one could go into my outlook diary, look at the meeting and assume they could double book or bump my meeting (people it was that deep!) It might seem minor, but those 20 minutes can work wonders by lowering your heart rate and your blood pressure in a way that can feel truly refreshing. Sometimes that's all you need to see your way through a challenging situation, or to get a fresh perspective on a challenge you've been wrestling.

6. **Identify your real stressors** – In our effort to make a good impression, show our capabilities, get the job, or people we apply our own self stressors. So, before you really frustrate yourself, stop and consider how much it really matters.

    - *Will it matter in 3 days?* If not, then it's probably not worth spending any more time on. Find a quick resolution and let it go.
    - *Will it matter in 3 months?* If yes, this indicates importance and longer-term impact, so it's probably worth a time investment.
    - *Will it matter in 3 years?* If yes, then it is essential in your life and deserves special attention. These are usually the big ones—relationships, happiness and work that makes a

difference. Make time for these because they rarely show up as urgent items on your to-do list.

If work seems overwhelming, stop and take another look. Is the frustration temporary? What can you do for yourself? It may be everything from being kinder to yourself, managing your time differently or even changing jobs.

7. **Seek real support** - Often when we're feeling stretched, there's nothing like a good old vent to colleagues, friends or family. Whingeing or complaining about our challenges can seem like a welcome relief but it's often short-lived solution. Your stressor is still there, and continuous complaining can make you feel even worse - like a helpless, irate victim. Instead, ask those around you to help you figure out how to reduce your overwhelm: get their support to help you figure out how to achieve the previous points. Ask them for any insights or advice they have about what's worked for them. Involving others in resolving your overload will ultimately be more satisfying for both of you - and far more useful.

8. **Get comfortable saying no.** – Who knew that such a small word held so much power? Learning how to say a diplomatic no (with a smile) can be life-saving. Quite often the women I coach who are the most overwhelmed simply don't know how or aren't willing to set reasonable boundaries for themselves, and so end up over committing themselves, then failing to accomplish what they want leading them to feel like a failure. Whenever someone makes a request of you, before you say yes, think about whether or not you can actually deliver on the commitment you'd be making, without sacrificing other commitments or leaving

yourself under unnecessary pressure. Phrase how you say no, don't just come out with a hard NO. Cushion what you're about to say. Instead of saying 'No, I don't have time for that' or 'No, that's not my job', take a more tactful approach to explaining your reason. Something like 'I would be love to work on that project, but I've got two deadlines coming up, and I don't think I would be able to work on it this week'.

9. **Am I surrounded by Energy Suckers?** - Energy Suckers (a.k.a Negative Nancies, Debbie Downers and Miserable Mikes). These are the people who find the perpetual cloud and put a dampener on any occasion. If you can't cut them out of your life entirely, turn your interactions with them into a game. When my neighbor says, "I hate this foul weather!" I say, "Isn't it great? It means I don't have to wash my car!"

There will always be an increasing number of demands placed on your time. Learning how to manage these demands rather than being overwhelmed by them is a great skill and one that will help to ensure your success in the long term. One key note, if you have exhausted all your options, and you are still struggling, then it might be worth looking for a new job if that's your core stressor, whilst it doesn't make you ill (right now) it can erode your confidence in your own abilities, which then makes it harder to leave and find another job. So, don't leave an important decision hanging too long.

This woman can self-reflection questions;

- At what times/circumstances do you mostly experience feel overwhelm?
- How do you know you're operating in the overwhelmed mode? How do you define it?

- Look at you workload right now, what must be done today and this week?
    o Now ask yourself, what's the best use of your time right now?
    o What steps could you take to prioritize your workload?
    o What are you doing now that someone else could do or at least help with?
- What areas in your life/job could you delegate or outsource on a longer-term basis?
- Who could you talk about how you're feeling?

"Sometimes when you're overwhelmed by a situation - when you're in the darkest of darkness - that's when your priorities are reordered."
Phoebe Snow

13. This Woman Can... manage the office bully!

Patricia was well respected manager by her team. She had been with her current company for almost 20 years and was the go-to person in her small business. As part of a larger organization, she managed a small isolated team and often felt overly stretched and taken for granted. Recently, her head office had provided much needed additional support via a secondment. However, Patricia felt that Cheryl – the secondee was anything but supportive! "She seems to be conspiring to make my life miserable. She bitches about me behind my back" (A colleague in another market had told Patricia about all the disparaging comments Cheryl had made about her). Cheryl was undermining Patricia by omitting her from important internal emails and meeting invitations, as well as doing petty things like updating their Boss on actions without her. Even worse because of Patricia's remote location, she didn't have the opportunity to build a relationship with their respective Boss as Cheryl did because she had worked in the same office.

Patricia was concerned, "Cheryl is twenty years my junior and I know I'm supposed to take the higher ground but if I admonish her I'm concerned it'd look like sour grapes. It's been going on since she joined the firm twelve months ago. I just want to get on with my job but get so distracted by her scheming and feel utterly paranoid and confused. Can I do anything?"

It doesn't matter what age or gender; what Patricia was describing was bullying and it's probably more common than you realize and according to research women tend to bully more women than men.

Bullying can occur in many forms including by email and phone, through deliberate exclusion and avoidance (as Patricia was experiencing); it can be personal or related to work activities. Workplace bullying is also not carried out by supervisors and superiors alone, but also by co-workers. In all cases, it is a form of power struggle. Whilst you may not realize or class it as such, most of us will face some kind of workplace bullying in our life time and with so many nuances it can be difficult to define and often the reason why it's not widely reported. Plus, women often do not feel comfortable talking about it or sharing it, because of how they'll be perceived as "weak", "overreacting" or "misconstruing".

Bullies also come in many shapes;

The Prankster - They think they're funny and are always having a laugh at someone else's expense. Yes, the first joke can be funny but if it's on constant replay and you're the butt of the joke every time it can quickly get incredibly tiresome and come across as mean. Not every prankster is a bully, but if you feel you have to stay on the right side of them all the time to avoid being the joke victim – then they're creating a thin line.

The Saboteur - Think of Cheryl - the back stabbers who make your job harder than it has to be, and find ways to prevent you from succeeding – they often smile in your face which makes it even worse. You think they're a trusted colleague, and don't realize they're poisoning the relationship by misremembering or omitting details, or pushing you out of important projects or calls so they can take credit for your work or ideas.

The Constant Critic - Haters, critics – call them what them what you like but they're always, always quick to find fault and are always quick with the criticism. They'll hold their victims to irrational or impossible standards, finding any and every all flaw in your work. They're not about letting you, your colleagues or your boss know about it.

The Cliques – We know all these – often The Mean Girls Clique – they find safety in numbers, working together to shut you out and make you feel downright uncomfortable.

The Side Eyers - They're the ones always glaring at you, looking you up, down and sideways. They don't hide their disdain and are constantly judging you ... hard. No matter what you say, the expression on their face says you were talking shit, because they see you as their competition, their nemesis even if you don't really know them or work in a different department.

The Freezers – Like the Cliques, but operate as the company gatekeeper, they accidently on purpose exclude you and others from social events, like lunches or happy hours, so that their targets never quite feel like they fit in. The freezers can also be highly competitive by intentionally excluding you from briefings and meetings.

The Big Mouth – We see you, every office has at least one of these (and consider yourself lucky if you only have!) They're the ones who are always have something to say, the biggest mouth in the room, so loud it always seems as if they're shouting. They're loud, over the top, obnoxious and humiliate others – by either being overtly rude or speaking over them in meetings (or both) so as to dismiss what they're saying.

The Gossip – The Big mouth and the Constant Critic are obvious with their bully tactics and you can see them coming, but the wily Gossips are content to work behind closed doors. They'll whisper in the break room and spread rumors on the lunch runs. Sometimes its personal stuff, sometimes it's performance-related, sometimes just hearsay – all are hurtful and can damage reputations.

The Puppet Master - The puppet master comes in many forms. It could be the sales manager who treats his team like pledges to be hazed, or it could be the call center team leader lording over a game of musical chairs in which reps compete for the chance to go home early. It can even be boss who makes you bring him or her coffee every day. There's nothing wrong with a little healthy competition; it can even be good for some teams and functions. But you should never feel like you're doing something for your boss' amusement.

The Attention Seeker - This type of bully wants to be the center of the action at all times. They'll do everything to get on their Boss's good side through consistent flattery aka butt-kissing and can even come appear kind and helpful to their peers – especially the newer employees who haven't learnt about them. But if they don't get the right amount of attention, they can quickly turn on you. They're often overly dramatic and relate everything to something that's going wrong in their own lives to gain sympathy and control. These bullies also have a tendency to coax personal info out of new employees – to use as ammunition against them later.

The Oracle – The Oracle sees themselves as absolutely indispensable and expects recognition for everything. But Oracles aren't usually very good at their job. So, to compensate, they spend a lot of their time watching more competent workers and looking for areas of skilled workers' performance to complain about. They'll demand that everything is done their way – even when there are better ways of doing things because they believe their way is only way. They're automatically opposed to others' ideas, and will do everything in their power to prevent changes to their work processes.

It's important to note that your bully maybe one or a combination of the bully types but the activities they subject you to are definitely not one-off events – that's harassment.

Bullying is deliberately intended to dominate, cause distress and fear in the intended victim. Bullying often happens in private settings and by a person in authority (but not exclusively hence the popularity of the Mean Girl cliques) and it can be difficult to find material evidence to prove that bullying tactics are taking place. What I do know, is that bullying doesn't happen "by accident", it's a deliberate action, and even though perpetrators might say they "meant no harm" "they were only joking" when reprimanded, bullying often involves a planned campaign by the bully with the likelihood of negative outcome for the bullied.

Now I'm not going to tackle employment law or organizational cultures (but I will stress it is an organization's responsibility to respond to the needs of its employees) – but if you are suffering in silence, or feeling ashamed for 'letting bullying happen to you' I hope these few tips will encourage you to take some action.

Record, record, record – Bullying tactics such as the ones Cheryl employed is a form of gaslighting – a method of psychological abuse that causes a person to question their self-worth and sanity. Keep a written record of who said or did what, and when. The frequency and pattern of the incidents you record will be strong evidence of the bullying you're experiencing, and will make it challenging for a bully to deny when they're confronted.

Be informed not in denial - If you are unsure or need convincing that you're experiencing bullying, find out more information to understand more about your bullies' behavior and ways in which you can respond effectively. Find out about your employer's approach to bullying and harassment, what does your company handbook say, who can you talk to? Feeling knowledgeable will help you feel more in control and understand your options in dealing with the situation.

Speak up - Talk to your colleagues, have they witnessed or experienced any of the incidents you've been subjected to? If they have, their evidence will prove invaluable to you if you need to escalate a complaint. Knowing you're not alone may help you collectively address the problem

Build a support network – At home, at work to boost your confidence and resilience. Find colleagues who will support your fight against the bullies. I can feel you cringe as you read this, you don't want to involve anyone else and conversely people shy away of being involved but if you can – seek to reinforce positive relationships with others in the office and make the most of friendships outside work.

Speak to your boss – This is a must – a good Boss will want to deal with the situation. Plan the meeting when you're calm and collected and have all your evidence – your 'incident and evidence from others in the office if it's available. If you're worried about being emotional in the meeting (don't be, you're allowed to be), if you don't think you'll be able to get all points across make notes beforehand and practice your key points to ensure you don't forget to mention anything important. Focus on how the bullies' behavior has affected you and on making your case as strong as possible.

Complaint unresolved? – Be prepared to escalate if the bullying continues and you feel your boss hasn't done anything about it, or their solution isn't effective (your boss could be inadvertently enabling your bullies' behavior), you should escalate a complaint internally by following your employer's internal procedures – usually via your HR department who should give you information about how to do this. If after all this it's still unresolved then you'd have to investigate your external options – i.e. Trade Unions, Labor Departments etc. depending on your country's employment law framework.

This woman can self-reflection questions;

- If you feel you're a victim of bullying, what leading you to suspect it?
- What options are available to you to address the problem?
- What actions have you taken to address the problem?
- Who could you talk to about your situation?

"I realized that bullying never has to do with you. It's the bully who's insecure."
Shay Mitchell

14. This Woman Can... be in control of her personal development.

Angie had decided to bite the bullet and contract me as her coach, she felt she'd been forced to do something different as her career wasn't going as planned. She was ambitious and knew she wanted to step into a leadership role. She'd applied for three entry level management roles internally over the past six months but hadn't been successful, she didn't even get to interview stage on her last application and couldn't work out why. As far as she was concerned, she had a good degree, she knew the business, she was well liked and friendly, plus she'd been with the company seven years, surely it was her time now?

This was our second session, after our first meeting I'd given her some homework - request feedback from the interviewing managers and HR to gain some understanding on why her application was unsuccessful and look at potential personal development areas.

Angie had been resistant in undertaking the task, she already had qualifications so what more did she need in order to take the next step in her career?

Personal development is an often used but rarely explained term. It doesn't stop because you completed formal education, it doesn't stop because you're older, it's not just further education e.g. university, training courses, coaching etc. In essence it's about investing in yourself so that you can manage yourself effectively no matter what life throws at you.

Personal development allows you to be proactive about your future rather than waiting for it happen. Whatever stage you're at in your life it should be a priority because;

- **It forces you out of your comfort zone** – Looking at Angie's situation, there were areas she needed to improve to progress her career, but she was in denial and wouldn't accept there were improvement areas. Proactively confronting these areas and improving on them would push her out of her complacency comfort zone allowing for growth and improved skills.
- **It develops your strengths** - Having an idea or a development plan can also help you to develop your strengths. By taking time to focus on nurturing and using your strengths more, you go from being good at something to being excellent at it.
- **It boosts your confidence** – Being in control of the decision to improve your skills instills confidence. Once you have achieved your goal, gained another skill or developed certain areas of your life, you automatically feel better about yourself ergo more development = more confidence!
- **It improves your self-awareness** – you're forced to take a long, hard, honest look at the areas of your life that need improvement. Through this process, you get to know who you really are, what your true values are, and where you would like to go in life.
- **It provides clarity** - If you're struggling with a career choice, starting up a new business, or simply need some help navigating your way through life; personal development can be a way to help you find solutions and understand new concepts.

In the business world, we know that no two workplaces, situations, crises, or scenarios are the same. Additionally, no two successful people are the same and their route to success followed different paths however, the key denominator is their attitude to self-development and their constant focus on working to improve themselves and their situations.

A successful person;

- Embraces their own personal development.
- Use every situation as learning opportunity.
- Understands that there's always an opportunity to learn even from their mistakes.
- Engages new people with an open mind.
- Focuses on the experience and not necessarily the result.
- Is open to try take a risk and constantly try new challenges.

One of the best ways to start your self-development is to prioritize your personal and professional goals. It is impossible to do everything, so it is important to make a list and make choices. That's where your personal development plan comes into play.

Having a written plan focused on your development activities is significant. It enables you place some real focus on what you need and acts as both a reminder and guide for the goals you've set for yourself. So, here are my top tips for developing your personal development plan.

1. Define what makes a great leader / accountant / engineer

Draw inspiration from persons you admire both in your personal life or the world around you, corporate or otherwise. Identify those skills or qualities you think make up the traits, competencies, abilities and experience of the role you'd like emulate.

2. Take a self-assessment

Identify your core characteristics or personality traits such "conscientious" "focused," and "driven." There are lots of free tests online such as the Myers-Briggs Type Indicator (MBTI) or StrengthsFinder. Alternatively, ask your friends, peers, colleagues and family to write down words they'd use to describe you. This will give you more insight into your personal style and you'll be able to better answer the "Who am I?" aspect of the personal development process.

3. Know your core values

Now that you've identified your core characteristics, it's time to identify your core values. These are the principles you use to make decisions that define your integrity and guide your ethics. They are the things that help you weigh choices in life, and are typically unwavering.

4. Draft your personal vision statement

A personal vision statement reflects your personal traits and core values. It seeks to answer the question, "Who am I and what is my calling?"

Within this you focus on the following points:

- What you want to be (in terms of character traits – refer to your self-assessment!)
- What you want to achieve or contribute
- The principles/values you use to make decisions, big and small

The personal vision statement will become your physical reminder of where you've been, where you are, and where you want to go. By outlining your vision, you will have something to look back on when it comes time to develop your goals and write an action plan.

Once you've written your personal statement, ask yourself the following:

- Does this represent who I stand for?
- Are direction, purpose, and motivation signaled in this statement?
- Is this an accurate portrait of who I want to be?
- Does this inspire me?

Nothing is set in stone. Your personal statement will and should evolve over time. It should reflect where you are now and where you hope to go.

5. Analyze what others think of you

This is key, if you aspire to be in a leadership role, you have an additional step in your plan. At this point you've dug deep to identify and understand your traits and drivers. However, being successful leader isn't just about what you think makes an effective leader. You also have to think about, do people want to work for you? As a leader, chances are you will have people who work for you and you need to know what are you like as a manager or as a leader? It can't just be that you are great at managing up, or your boss thinks you're fabulous. It's important to think through, what do your direct reports think, what do your peers think in terms of your effectiveness, and what do your leaders think about you in terms of your effectiveness?

So, check if the personality traits, core values, and personal mission statement you settled on in align with what others currently think of both you and leaders in general, ask yourself the following:

- What do you want your employees and co-workers to say about you when you are not in the room?
- What do they actually say? (You might know the answer already but if not, ask a trusted peer.)
- How do others currently perceive you?
- Do you care about others' perceptions of you?
- What are the expectations for professionalism and leadership in your field?

If your personal assessment doesn't align with the answers to these questions, are you capable of making the changes required to your image, ethics, values etc.? If so, are the benefits worth the costs (mental, emotional, physiological, and physical) to change? Do you even want to make the change?

Your answers will serve as a leveler to all the work you did prior to this step. You'll be able to identify the gaps in what/where you want to be vs. what people already think you are or need to be. You'll be able to pinpoint exactly where you need to improve, which will help with the next step.

6. Identify your current and missing skills

Now you've defined the qualities for your career vision; your own personality traits, core values, and personal vision; plus, a list of what other people think of you. All this reflection allows you to accomplish your next step: Expanding and further defining the skills you need to become your definition of great in your chosen career goal.

- Start by identifying the skills you already possess. Skills are different than traits: Skills can be taught (e.g. Excel, communication, delegating, etc.). Traits are natural abilities that last a lifetime (e.g. thoughtful, risk-adverse, introverted, etc.).
- Consider your personal, interpersonal, group and technical skills.

Once you've made your list, mark each item you consider a strength or those you consider an area for development. If you're unsure, ask a mentor, friends, and/or colleagues to offer their insights.

Finally, cross reference the skills you identified with the lists you made of "skills all great XXX have" and "the skills others think I have (or lack)." Ask yourself, "Where arethere gaps in which I need to improve?"

Note that you don't need to embody every single trait. Neither do you need to improve on every single skill others think you need. Focus on your core areas by cross referencing them with your core values and personal mission statement. If the skills don't align with these, deprioritize or lose them altogether.

Finally prioritize your list of skills in descending order by "need development" and strengths, it's now time to make some goals.

7. Goal setting

This is where all your hard work of self-analysis and research come into play. Using the prioritized personal skills list you developed, define 2–3 development goals that will stretch and challenge you and 1–2 manageable goals that will help you achieve each of your reach goals.

Adhering to the SMART acronym:

Specific: Ask who, what, where, when, why, and which

Measurable: How you'll know you've achieved the goal - "How much?", "How many?"

Attainable: You have a establish a realistic time frame; consider what conditions would have to exist to accomplish the goal

Realistic: The set are things you are willing and able to work toward — things you believe can be accomplished and that you actually want to accomplish

Timely: They'll be completed within a specific time frame

8. Write that action plan – and stick to it!

Your action plan lays out the specific steps you'll take, the resources you'll use, and the support system you'll need to reach your goals. For each goal note, define the following;

- Specific actions you need to take
- Resources to aid development - including any personal training
- Timelines

Then, put them in order of importance and/or time it will take to achieve said goals. Sometimes, the most difficult of this process is actually executing your actions, life can get in the way. So, depending on the action, physically allocate some personal development time in your calendar;

- You may be an early riser - dedicate 30 minutes for yourself.

- Walker/runner? - listen to podcasts that will aid your goal achievement
- At work – earmark one or two lunch hours to get out and focus on yourself.

Ultimately, if you want it hard enough, you'll find a way to make it work, excuses are your self- saboteur. You have to be prepared to consider what are the ways you're going to reinvent yourself, either small or big, to make sure you can succeed?

This is now your personal road map for achieving your goals. Remember: your personal development plan represents where you are now and where you hope to go. Revisit your plan often, make it a priority to update it and amend as needed, so that it reflects where you are on both your personal and career journey. As well as enabling you to grow as a person whilst growing your skills, improving your self-awareness, and boosting your confidence.

This woman can self-reflection questions;

- When was the last time you reviewed your personal development?
- What motivates you in your career choice?
- If you knew you couldn't fail, what career would you pursue and why?

"It takes courage for a leader to identify and confront self-imposed barriers, to put in place the personal strategies required to unleash the energy, innovation, and commitment to self-development."
Frances Hesselbein

15. This Woman Can... believe she's good enough!

The Fear of "Not Being Good Enough - It's something we all struggle with at some point in our life, but it doesn't have to be that way. I recall standing up at a women's networking event, an event that gives you 90 seconds to tell your story on a pre-determined topic. I hadn't planned it, I wrote my piece on my phone during the intermission, swallowed my fear and for want of a better word performed. I'd never shared my personal story, as I feared no one would what to hear it, who did I think I was and the biggie – I'm not good enough to do this!!!

There's a logical fallacy that underlies the fear of not being good enough – but that logic falls through because certain underlying assumptions that would make it true, just aren't there. The biggest one is that "enough" can be clearly defined. Consider this question: How would you even begin to define what qualifies as "good enough"?

You can probably list several ideas: I'd be good enough if "I...didn't shout at my kids", "made more money", "lost 10 pounds", "actually committed deeply to my career", "stopped procrastinating..." but you'll find the goalpost will always move as the definition of enough is subjective. The notion of being good enough lies in everybody's individual opinion.

Usually, the source of this thought is our inner critic or inner mean girl. She can be cruel, but she actually doesn't have bad intentions. In fact, she's trying to protect you, look out for you, keep you safe and motivate you to survive. But the over protective security guard, stops you from going for what you want in life

I work to overcome the feeling of being "not being good enough" by using the following strategies that might work for you as well.

Make a Decision - As individuals, we have the incredible power to decide that we are, in fact, good enough. You are the person who owns the sole key to your self-worth, which governs what you do. In order to achieve the feeling of being good enough, you must first believe it.

If you choose not to do so, then no one else can do it for you. Write it down and say it to yourself. When you make the choice, you become the Boss and you are back in power. You hold that key, yet we often forget that you do. So, remind yourself that when you feel imperfect, you've chosen to be imperfect. You must believe -- truly believe -- that you are good enough, which will allow you to let go of your quest for perfection.

Emphasize the Positive - How often do you quickly dismiss something you did well? Do you allow yourself to recognize and accept praise from others and feel that you deserve it? When someone tells me I look good, immediately find the "prop" that made look good – the lip gloss, different hair and not own that the props are just there to enhance me, so yes, I do look good. The frequency of this is likely much less than the amount of time you spend dwelling on something you did wrong or even sub-par. Do you recognize criticism and feel that you deserve it much more than praise?

Always remember that you're on your own side, always.

Redefine Perfect - During my first year as a mature student at University, I failed my first math's-based exam. I had prepared so much for the exam knowing that math and numbers were my Achilles heel. I can still remember the feeling when I saw the fail score on my exam and began to doubt whether I even belonged at University. I mean what was a divorced, single parent even doing at school, this was a young person's game? I called my Mom who gave me a good talking to and I buckled down and re took the exam in summer, knowing that if I didn't my dreams of getting a degree would be over. Ultimately, I graduated and went on to gain a MA with distinction and I credit that exam for my academic success.

My challenge had been that I had only focused on being "perfect" going into University and that exam served as my wakeup call.

Perfect was no longer what I wanted. Instead, my first goal distilled into simply passing my exams. When the threat of perfection was lifted, so was the pressure and anxiety I felt while preparing for and taking exams. I also re-examined my expectations. What was my real objective? The best grades in the class? Know the topic inside out? No, I wanted to gain a degree. That was the overall goal.

By focusing on progress and perfection, releasing yourself from the self-imposed pressure of perfection, you release the corresponding anxiety and allow yourself to perform up to your abilities.

Uncover the True Message - When you experience not being good enough as a result of interaction with other people, it's because you have a tendency to personalize everything they say or don't say, and take it to heart. But it doesn't have to be. It's not all about you. Actions speak louder than words. You probably have heard this saying many times before. The way in which they interact with you is according to their dictionary of how love is expressed, not yours. So, don't expect them to live life according to your terms.

Practice Self-Love - Did you know that you're very special? There is no other person in this world like you. You deserve to be loved not only by those around you but by the most important person in your life — YOU. Practicing self-love can be challenging for many of us, especially in times when we face serious challenges. It's not about being self-absorbed or narcissistic, it's about getting in touch with ourselves, our well-being and our happiness.

What's Your Authentic Mission in Life? - Why is it that you still find yourself rushing to prove to others that you deserve to be loved and to love? Why? It's powerful question. We spend too much time trying to figure out why that we forget that it doesn't really matter. It's rarely about why.

If you rely on somebody's validation of your success, you will never be free. You will never be able to fully realize your passion. It will be so easy for anyone to derail you off your path. The next time you are uncertain about your success -- reflect back on why you are in this business, this relationship, or this career in the first place.

Love Yourself for Who You Are - Sometimes you don't feel good enough because you compare yourself to other people. Stop this. You need to remember that you bring so much to the table and the world would be so different without you. Love yourself for who you are. You deserve to celebrate being you.

When you have these feelings or thoughts of not being good enough in any aspect of your life, try to always remind yourself to love yourself for who you really are. Try to name at least three things that love about yourself and that you're proud of being good at. Understand that it's simply impossible for a person to be everything to everyone and to be perfect at everything. You will create obstacles by focusing on what you are not, you just reinforce the limiting belief of not being good enough and worthy of people's attention.

Play by Your Own Rules - From my experience coaching women, I can confidently say that you can't force people to see from your own reality. We all have our own reality and each reality is valid. Accept that you can't control people or even change their behavior by telling them not to do something and focus on your own reality.

Don't Use Self-Deprecating Language - It's time to believe in your words when you communicate them to other people. You don't want to disregard your thoughts just because you don't think they're good enough or afraid that someone else won't like them. "Have a point of view. Don't use minimizing phrases like 'I was just thinking …' or 'I could be wrong, but …' make statements rather than asking questions. Cut all of that self-deprecating language out of your vocabulary and simply say what you want to say – and do it with confidence

Expose Yourself to The Activity You Fear - This is a case of feel the fear and do it anyway. One of the best ways to get over your fear of not being good enough is by actually doing the thing that you fear the most. Exposing yourself to your fear (and gradual increase of exposure) can help alleviate fear and anxiety around feeling inadequate. When you fear you won't perform 'well enough' or 'perfectly' do it anyway. This, in turn, will help to boost self-esteem and identity,"

So, we could explore this topic for a lot longer but the definition of enough can vary for everyone but here is the truth about what will make you start feeling good enough:

No longer assuming that you're not good enough.

No longer turning your back to the fact that you are good enough.

No longer trying to find evidence that you are good enough.

This woman can self-reflection questions;

- What is your definition of 'good enough' and 'not good enough'?
- Can you really define these?
- What strategies will you use to quiet you inner critic/mean girl?

"Never think your life isn't good enough. You only have one, so enjoy every minute."
Iskra Lawrence

16. This Woman Can... exit gracefully!

Let me update you on Angie from the previous chapter on personal development. She had successfully applied all her coaching actions and after six months had landed herself a new job which raised a new area of anxiety for her – "How do I hand in my resignation?"

Lots of women fret about their first day at a new job and prep for it like it's their first day of school, they're concerned that they'll fit I and get along with their colleagues and if it's a promotion that they live up to expectations. However, I think that just as much attention is needed when you hand in your notice. I'm not talking about the exit interview you may have to complete, oh no there's a lot more to it than that. Just as you prepare to start a job, there's a way to exit an organization and that preparation starts before you leave, way before the exit interview.

For those of us who have spent longer in the employee zone, we can probably recall stories of spectacular exits that went down in company folklore.

With the 6 degrees of separation phenomenon (especially in a small town or a small island such as I where I live) I can't stress how important it is not to burn bridges and the need to plan your exit strategy, leave positive impression, not burn too many bridges and for those of you specifically in leadership not leave the business in a tight spot. I've coached women who would have stayed in their current job rather than submit their resignation, exiting gracefully and learning how to not let fear stop you from taking an opportunity is essential.

Depending on the seniority of your role there may some additional steps, so I'll point out if applicable.

Tell the right people first aka tell no-one until you've told your Boss – I can't tell you how annoying it is to hear of someone's departure via the organizational grapevine personally I find it disrespectful and a slap in the face especially if you've built a good relationship with the employee. Not only is it irritating, but you've lost your chance to manage the narrative of why you're leaving. Once word of your quitting has become office gossip, it can take a life of its own.

I know you're excited by the new job and really, really want to divulge your secret to a work colleague — it's a big deal and it's only natural to want to talk it through with your inner circle. But fight the temptation and do the right thing by telling your manager first.

Pull up your big girls' panties, go into your manager's office with a clear story line about why you are resigning, when you want your last day to be and how you want the news communicated to others in the company. If you're a manager then last point is particularly important, as there may be organizational or political issues to manage, and your manager may need to alert HR and others in the company before word gets out. You may want to tell your team.

Whatever the case, work with your Boss to clarify the timing and public details surrounding your decision so that you're both singing the same song.

That way nobody can ever say they heard anything different.

But they want to offer me more money/a promotion/more responsibility... - When an organization is about to lose their star player all the goodies start appearing – the counteroffer! It's flattering, all the thoughts start running through your head – "they love me, they don't me want to leave, they can't operate without me" we all want to feel essential to a company, to feel that it can't run without us—which is why a counteroffer can be so appealing. But as you'd have guessed I have some thoughts about this;

- First of all, this is not the beginning of a negotiation. So, remain confident in your decision to leave. If the company makes you a counteroffer, be realistic about why your boss is making it.
- True that you maybe a vital pillar of the organization, however it's more probable that your boss would rather throw money at the situation rather than deal with the disruption caused by your departure.
- More importantly, think back to your reason for leaving, more money won't fix anything more than more money – which in my experience isn't usually the reason you had for leaving. Additionally, if they really valued you, why did you have to go through the turmoil of finding another job before they recognized your worth to the company? If there are other reasons why you want to leave, they most likely haven't changed, so make sure you really weigh the pros and cons of staying.
- Bear in mind too that if you do accept the counteroffer, you need to be prepared to recommit to your current job for a solid year—no more job hunting. Fully commit!

Continue to work, work, work, work, work - Just because you've handed your notice in doesn't mean all bets are off. You're not on a subsidized staycation. You're not on extended sick leave. You don't have additional holiday. What you do have is an active contract and a job you're still being paid to do, so do it. Tempting as it may be (and possibly well deserved), focus on protecting the reputation you've worked so hard to build and do the exact opposite.

As you transition out, you want people walking around the office wondering what the hell is going to happen to the business after you leave. You want to be the superstar around the office no one thinks they can live without. Stay on top of your responsibilities. Remember that you're accountable for your work until you walk out the door on your last day. There's an added bonus; it's not uncommon for star employees to be hired back on better terms or even find yourself being employed by someone you worked for in another organization. That only happens if you treat your notice period more seriously than you when you started.

Work your notice - Simple, whatever your contractual notice period is adhere to it unless you and your boss have come to a mutual agreement e.g. forfeited holiday as part of your notice period, received pay in lieu of notice etc. If you're in a position to give extra time (and your boss is in agreement) then it's a nice gesture, your boss will be appreciative that you're leaving plenty of time to wrap up your projects.

A little side note: If you've seen your company escort employees right out the door once they give their resignation, don't give any more than your contracted notice. In this situation, it's best to prepare yourself well in advance by tying up loose ends before making your announcement.

Leave them wanting more – No matter what your relationship has been with your exiting organization, please, please, please leave on a high note. Just as first impressions count, the final impression shapes how people remember you. After all the hard work and time, you've put into doing a great job, you don't want the lasting memory to be "Do you remember when Janice…" (Insert outrageous act here)! All your great work secures a positive memory in the minds of everybody you worked with. The memory you are aiming to create is of a woman who is smart, valuable, knows her stuff, fun and ultimately "we'd hire her again".

Plus, remember in the age of social media that final impressions can last much longer than your last day of work and can be a double edge sword! On one hand you have the opportunity to represent your employer and stay in touch with your former colleagues forever. On the other, that time you did a wheel spin in the car park, middle finger in the air, screaming f*ck you (true story) can return to haunt you time and again by providing the reference you really didn't want.

Return to these principles again and again, and you'll find that your network and reputation will last much longer than your role.

If you don't have something nice to say, don't say anything at all – Yes, you're happy, but remember your colleagues are still employed! Calling it quits doesn't give you free rein to bad talk the company or a colleague—to anyone. Be modest. Don't alienate your colleagues by bragging or chattering incessantly about your awesome new gig.

Remember, you may think there's no way on earth you're ever going to see this person again but sure enough they show up five years later in a different capacity even worse as your boss! The same applies to any remarks on social media – you don't want to become viral for the wrong reasons.

I've always adopted the popular break up manta "it's not you, it's me". Translation: You guys are great. It's nothing personal, it's just time for me to move on.

Wrap things up - While you're fantasizing about your fabulous new job and how lost people will be without you, your boss is working out how he's going to keep everything running. So, in your final days you can still leave a great impression by doing the following;

- Whatever you're working on, finish it - even if it requires more hours than you would like to spend on your current job, it's your responsibility to not leave any loose ends. There's nothing better to create confusion in an organization than an unfinished project with no instructions as to how to complete. Expect numerous calls for help or gossip about how wrong it was for you to leave. If it really can't be wrapped up during your notice period, draft a solid handover plan outlining all of your pending projects, your recommendations for wrapping them up and specific employees you plan to brief to ensure the job gets done.

- This isn't just for the sake of your replacement, but because it leaves your professional reputation in tact on a high and positive note. Nothing shows gratitude and accountability like a job that's done well—and finished.

- If time allows, offer to train your replacement. We all know that your boss doesn't know your job as well as you do. You have all the secret work arounds and connection that enable you to deliver the fabulous job you did, so, if you can help with this part of your exit, then you're winning points all around. Offer to help recruit your replacement, sift through resumes, sit in on interviews, work with the new employee, or create a training manual for your job. It will go a long way to leaving a good impression once you're gone.

When's the best time to leave? – That really is up to you and sometimes you don't have a choice but there may be some considerations;

- If you're a people manager with team responsibilities, you may not want to leave your team in the lurch and so delay departure until you've identified/trained your successor so there's some continuity.
- You're in the middle of a significant project that can would leave an organization in a detrimental position and if you abandoned mid-point may damage your reputation.
- If your company gives an annual or holiday bonus, you may not be entitled to receive it if you've handed in your notice in, so bear that in mind and maybe hold off until afterward to ensure you get your extra pay if that's important to you.
- If you or your family have a tuition loan provided by your employer, you could lose it if you quit while you or your dependents are still in school. Check the small print in your tuition reimbursement plan and plan accordingly.
- If you're undergoing medical treatment and are utilizing your company medical plan, before you resign, check to see what options are available – can you take over your insurance payment to ensure continuity in treatment?

Leave it alone, it's not yours - Don't take anything that doesn't belong to you. This includes office supplies and work material that was not developed by you personally. If it was developed by you e.g. a training program, an internal app etc. what does your contract say about intellectual property (items designed by you whilst contractually employed). As a general rule, an employer will own the intellectual property created by its employees in the course of their employment.

Pay it forward – When I was planning to move to the Caribbean, I knew the role I had wasn't my career peak, but I did know that one of my reportees would be great for the position with a little nurturing and guidance. As I hadn't made my emigration plans secret I shared my thoughts with both him and my Boss allowing me to act as a mentor, exposing him to situations and meetings he normally wouldn't attend due to seniority readying him to step up if he wanted the job. If you're in any position of seniority, there will always be people underneath you, it might be a formal or informal reporting relationship, but a good leader can spot talent. One of the best gifts you can give any colleague is value. Making other people look good is always going to make you look good, you have everything to gain by building your colleagues up and offering your help as you leave.

The example I gave is unusual, but there are other ways you can pay it forward. For instance, genuine (and kind) feedback on performance and reputation. You can pass on ideas and initiatives onto someone else, you know will benefit once followed through. You can use your leaving as an opportunity to discuss a colleague's career goals and if you get on with your boss you might even candidly share your experiences at the company, as long as it's productive. Whatever you do, look for the ways — big and small — that you might add value to your colleagues as you leave.

It's a totally selfless act, it doesn't cost you anything, but the payback is real. It's the kind of behavior we champion in all relationships especially professional ones, it builds lasting loyalty and deep appreciation. The same treatment we'd like to receive.

Repeat after me - exit interviews are not therapy sessions – That last meeting with HR can be a potential minefield, the one where you're asked to share your views about your employee experience. It can be tempting to unload about the company or share details about toxic colleagues, tread carefully – no matter what they tell you there's no such thing as anonymity or off-the-record comments. Think about, the purpose of the interview, it's to identify company flaws - HR absolutely can and will share what they heard in some format, so phrase your feedback constructively and if you can't say something positive say nothing. (If you're really feeling perturbed by something happening in your organization, don't wait until you're leaving, utilize prescribed channels to have it addressed not just for you but also to benefit your colleagues.)

That Boss you want to throw under the bus? No point, not only will they hear about it (which burns a bridge) but unless, they've committed a serious grievance such as sexual harassment, company fraud etc., it isn't likely that HR will actually be a position to penalize that person. Not saying you should lie, just be selective with your words, it's a smaller world than you think, and you never know when you're going to need or see these people again. At the very least, you may want someone at the company to act as a referee for you in the future.

The Departure email – It's customary in large organizations to send goodbye emails, you know the ones telling everybody in the global distribution list farewell. Not a big fan on the global part as unless you were the Chairman, not everyone knew or cared who you were. So, proceed with caution, as that pissy note you send could have the same impact as the social media post mentioned. I am however a fan of sending a more personalized note to colleagues who mattered to you and a more appreciative one to a Boss who made a difference. Ultimately, how you say goodbye is your choice, again just don't burn bridges.

Breathe, you did it! Be grateful, you're sitting pretty in your new job and still on speaking terms with all parties involved, well done you can take a breather and pat yourself on the back! Showing gratitude, manner and professionalism throughout the entire process will make sure they'll remember you fondly (whether or not you can say the same for them).

This woman can self-reflection questions;

- If you were to resign from your current role, what would do differently?
- Who have seen exit a business gracefully and what could you learn?
- How do you want people to remember you when you're no longer with your current organization?

"There's a trick to the Graceful Exit. It begins with the vision to recognize when a job, a life stage, a relationship is over - and to let go. It means leaving what's over without denying its value."
Ellen Goodman

17. This Woman Can... be strong enough to handle sexual harassment.

Annette worked with a mainly male technical team and sometimes her boss Bryan made comments to her about how well her uniform fitted her and how attractive she was. She had never responded when he made these comments just preferring to get on with her job. During her bi-annual appraisal, Annette highlighted her progress in the role and the targets that the department had achieved as a result of the activities she had executed. As part of the discussion Annette requested that she be considered for a pay increase based on her performance. Bryan told her he would consider her request and suggested that the two of them go out for dinner and drinks. Annette was hesitant and made it clear that she wanted to keep their relationship purely professional and would therefore prefer not to go out with him. Bryan stated that he understood. Annette followed up her request but was informed by Bryan that her request had been denied but if she could be more "co-operative" and work with him, he'd see if he could put a good word in for her with the powers that be. Annette asked what does "co-operative" mean, Bryan smiled and simply said "You work it out".

At our session Annette asks "Can he do that? I'm livid, surely my pay increase should be based purely on my performance, not him having drinks with him so he'll give the nod to his boss. I really don't feel comfortable with this; does it mean he'll only support my increase if I have dinner with him?"

We all know harassment exists but when it happens to you, especially if you are new in the workforce. It's deeply disturbing and often difficult to react in the appropriate manner. The less experience you have the more vexing it is to muster your internal resources. First, because it's shocking and second you want to be judged on your work and this totally flips your perceptions on so many levels. The good news is that we may have finally reached a tipping point that may shed even more awareness within the workplace, letting individuals know that their behavior will not be tolerated.

Let me stress that NO matter what – it is NOT ok for any man or woman to sexually harass any woman or a woman to harass a woman, a man to harass a man – you get the idea - it's equal opportunities.

Even though women have made some headway, we still get constant reminders of how male-dominated the business world is and why women who want to be successful need to learn how to navigate it, we can have all the university qualifications in this world but as women we have to learn how to thrive in this environment.

So, I know the definition of Sexual Harassment has probably beaten to death by now, but it doesn't hurt to recap on what it is and how it differs from non-sexual harassment? Sexual harassment is a form of discrimination and includes any uninvited comments, conduct, or behavior regarding sex, gender, or sexual orientation.

It doesn't matter who makes the offense - a manager, colleague, or even a non-employee like a client, contractor, or vendor, if the conduct creates a hostile work environment, makes you uncomfortable or interrupts your success, it is considered unlawful sexual harassment.

Sexual harassment isn't limited to making inappropriate advances. It includes any unwelcome verbal or physical behavior that creates a hostile work environment and when I say hostile I mean it makes you uncomfortable.

Examples include;

- Sharing sexually inappropriate images or videos, such as pornography
- Sending suggestive letters, notes, or e-mails - so the sharing of something you found funny on social media are a definite no, no.
- Displaying inappropriate sexual images or posters in the workplace ~ in the U.K. we had newspapers that had a topless model on page 3 of the paper every day and men used to pin them to their wall and joke about the women. I even recall them comparing female colleagues to the models. They only stopped publishing the page in 2015, so in the 21st century men still thought this was acceptable. No!
- Telling lewd or dirty jokes, or sharing sexual anecdotes or recounting an incident you saw on social media.
- Making inappropriate sexual gestures
- Staring in a sexually suggestive or offensive manner, or (wolf) whistling
- Making sexual comments about appearance, clothing, or body parts
- Inappropriate touching, including pinching, patting, rubbing, or purposefully brushing up against another person
- Asking sexual questions, such as questions about someone's sexual history or their sexual orientation ~ that's nobody's business but your own.
- Bartering for sexual favors e.g. I'll overlook a misdemeanor if you give me a kiss/have drinks with me/come to dinner etc.

- Making offensive comments about someone's sexual orientation or gender identity ~ whether I like men or women, is none of your damn business.

People are always finding new ways to exploit or harass so this list is in no way exhaustive ~ the key thing is if it makes you or anyone else around you feel uncomfortable, then it's sexual harassment.

So, what do you do if you feel sexually harassed?

When it comes to dealing with unwanted attentions or blatant harassment, the challenge is not only how to take the incident seriously but how to manage it successfully, so that there is minimal impact to your career or saps your confidence. Having been on both sides of the fence employer and the harassed - even if I didn't recognize it until after the fact. Here are a few things that have helped me along the way;

Don't sweat the small stuff - Part of working together every day with the same people includes joking around and, yes, even a bit of teasing and sometimes a little over familiarity. I'm sure there's been times you've heard men giving each other a hard time about each other's clothes or car, or even work? It's how men often relate to each other and it's typically not personal. Men don't cry or shut down; they either chupse (kiss their teeth) or give it back. Learn to do the same. And if you get good and clever at dishing it back, you might be surprised at the additional respect you gain.

Draw a hard line - Some joking and bantering is fun and tolerable; some isn't. When it isn't, call it out--immediately, put it in check, and shut it down. Completely change your demeanor, be direct, and make it very clear they've crossed a big line. It can be as simple as "OK, that wasn't funny" or as serious as "you are making me feel very uncomfortable right now, please stop." Even better if others are around to hear you.

Trust me--no individual wants to be the accused in a harassment situation and if you treat it seriously, the other person probably will too.

Rise above the haters - Sometimes it is personal and potentially damaging. I had a close friend Sharon a senior manager for a bank and she was responsible for business sales. She's really sharp, young, and very attractive. She had spent months devising a new strategy to attract new business and was presenting for the first time to an all-male team. It was a really different approach for the business and would significantly change how they did business recommendations too and she expected some tough questions. A male team member gave her the side eye, looking her up and down, obviously not listening and attempting to throw her off her stride. As she was speaking he interrupted and said to his colleague, "The first thing I think you need to do is get rid of the GIRL." Many would stumble in this situation, which is what he wanted, but Sharon thought "Oh, you want to test me? She stood up straighter looking even more gorgeous, looked him straight in the eyes, and shot back: "Well that's one option, or we can further examine the facts..." and went on to her presentation to the team.

The meeting ended with most of her recommendations being supported and a renewed respect for her from the rest of the team. The offending man was later disciplined for his bad behavior in the meeting. She wins big, he loses. I know it's easier said than done, but in most cases, you'll find that people don't want to see others harassed. Be confident in your intelligence and skills and rise above the idiots.

Don't shit where you eat - in other words don't mix business with pleasure - It's not something I've ever done as I think it can get complicated, but I have seen others get involved and it got very messy, very quickly. Dating someone at work can get complicated and lead to issues. Especially when you fallout and it becomes "he said, she said". I've seen incidents where persons have tried to extract revenge by dropping the other in the proverbial 'it' by claiming they've been harassed when previously they'd claimed their relationship had been consensual. I'm not saying harassment didn't take place, maybe it did and maybe it's someone they should have steered clear of in the first place. But main thing you have to think long and hard about whether or not a relationship at work is worth the risk. If it is, then keep your eyes open and be ready to handle the potential consequences.

Keep your head/Remember where you are - Work events are another mine field. I cannot tell you how many events especially when I was in the U.K. where I've seen alcohol get the better of people. They drink too much and end up snogging someone they've never ever consider on a sober day or even worse. I recall one event when a very senior manager was caught in a very compromising situation with a young employee, after the event she accused him of sexual assault which was taken seriously but she wasn't clear on what happened because of the alcohol inducement and until you can prove it, it's just an accusation. She ended up leaving her job and most likely not getting the help she needed.

Speak Up/Tell Now - Please, please, please say something anything ~ if you're truly feeling harassed, document it immediately and report it. If no one knows what's going on, no one can help you or do anything. If you're at work, talk to HR, talk to your Boss, talk to a colleague but please talk to someone. Because we tend to keep these things to ourselves we think no one will believe us but, in my experience, this won't have been the first-time a) they've dealt with similar situations and b) not the first time the harasser has done similar to someone else. Don't be afraid ~ think what's worse, saying something to someone who can help you or not saying something and continuing in silence with the situation? You should never have to endure harassment.

Harassment doesn't respect hierarchy - It's not just persons at the very top. The offender doesn't have to be the most senior in the business ~ it's anyone who has a perceived notion of power and wields it to inflict discomfort on others.

Don't quit - Don't give up your job, that's tantamount to giving in and you're not the offender.

Don't make excuses for the offender – I once conducted a sexual harassment investigation and the response to one of the questions were some of the most disturbing things I'd heard when asked about a male colleague's habit of making lewd jokes or passes at women in the workplace – "Oh that's just the way he is, he doesn't mean it" STOP IT. Just because that's what he's always done doesn't make it right. If it makes someone uncomfortable, then it's wrong.

So, if you're being harassed, how should you handle it?

I'm not an expert, but often the best technique, which most of us have learned in self-defense class, is to be direct and simply tell the person to stop, let the individual know they are harassing you, and you will report them as well as tell others including your supervisor and HR. Verbiage can be as simple as " you are making me feel very uncomfortable right now, please stop." That usually works and sometimes someone doesn't even realize they are making you uncomfortable. Make sure to write down the facts and keep a record if you decide to report it to HR. Documenting it is really, really important. Even just for your own sanity, keep careful notes and records of what happens and report it. If it's your boss, try going to his/her boss, you have to keep going up until you feel safe. The organization has to understand that this is the proper practice. Don't allow them to delegate the complaint back down, they must take responsibility at the level that it is brought, sometimes this can be a challenge because people are connected to each other (they're friends, related etc.) and want to cover/make excuses for each other. Then, not all companies have HR departments and not all HR people are effective! Dealing with it may not your most pleasant career experience, but don't stop, get it, get it.

If all else fails, you may need to be prepared to walk away from an opportunity or job. It's a tough decision but you have to take the best path forward for you.

This woman can self-reflection questions;

- Where can you seek advice in your organization if you're experiencing sexual harassment?

> "We must have zero tolerance for sexual harassment, even if the perpetrator is somebody we like and admire."
> Ana Navarro

18. This Woman Can... fight the fear of leadership!

I'll share a secret with you - I never wanted to become a CEO, let alone the first woman to hold the role in a male dominated industry in an adopted country. I had already emigrated to the Caribbean with a plan – that was to work for a few years, establish myself in my new country, slow down my work pace and semi retire! Why else would you move to a top vacation spot and work so hard that you never enjoy it?

Life however had other plans!

It happened soon after the regular shuffle of expatriate CEOs across the region. On my return from vacation, my Regional CEO requested that we meet for coffee prior to coming back into the office. Oh sh*t I thought what have I done? (You know you always feel guilty even when logic tells you you're innocent). The recent shuffle included my CEO which meant that CEO role in my country would be vacant and I was the only candidate for the job! The news made me cringe. I wasn't sure I wanted to run the show. I'd been with the organization for a number of years and had observed how the male CEOs not only acted but were treated – I wasn't sure that at my age whether I wanted to go through all that. But my mind rewound a conversation I'd had with a prior CEO as he was leaving to return to his home country, he was encouraging me to apply for his role, after all I was the one making him look good! I explained how I felt about the behaviors of prior CEO role models, how that wasn't my leadership style and if it that was what required then I couldn't do it. His response "Make the role your own" – simple!

It was a like lightbulb moment and it was at that point I said yes and was appointed the first female CEO in the Telecommunications industry for both Antigua and Montserrat. I lead the way that was natural to me and discovered I absolutely loved it. Power, as it turned out, looked and felt a lot different from the inside out than it did from outside in. It was exhilarating, rewarding, fun, and, rather than restricting, wonderfully freeing. I called the shots, my way.

That said being a leader is definitely not an easy job. A lot of women experience unconscious fears that physically stops them from taking steps in the leadership realm. For me it was the fear of having to change who I was. You may aspire to be a leader because;

- You think you can do a better job,
- You believe you're ready for leadership,
- You believe you've earned it by working hard or length of tenure.
- You may leadership thrust upon you!

But let me share something with you - leading people is a whole lot different from leading projects and it's different from *managing* people. It forces you to flex your capabilities and practice the art of contortionism. Leadership is what they don't tell you in the interview, read in the books or is unseen on TV - the changes when you become a leader are subtle. The expectations from all levels in your company will be different. What was once considered acceptable behavior is different. The relationships you have with your peers will be different. No one, I repeat no one gives you a playbook about what to expect and if they did it would still differ.

Those who find themselves in the role of a leader often find it overwhelming. For some, the fear of being a leader carries with it some very strong feelings and emotions. Some leaders do not find it easy to address their fear. In fact, some female leaders have never identified their fears and that can manifest itself in the "Bitch Boss" persona. Mastering any new skill usually requires some element of fear-domination. Leadership is no different.

One of my first roles as a newly appointed call center manager was to recruit new agents for the expansion of our successful outbound calling team. Now I'd had experience of recruiting agents, but we were tasked with recruiting (and training) 200 people within a six-month period whilst still covering staff attrition. Due to the sheer numbers involved, we knew that that number of experienced agents weren't readily available and essentially, we'd have to "grow our own". This meant identifying and adopting new recruitment strategies and being flexible and open to all ideas – nothing was scared. This was the first major recruitment drive for all of us so there were certainly some fears that had to be overcome. And we had to do so quickly, or suffer the consequences.

The first step in overcoming fear is being prepared. None of us knew how ready we were until we were tested in that recruitment challenge. During our first month of back to back assessment centers, long days and repetitive interviews, not one person hesitated to be part of the process. Instead we put our heads together, looked at the challenge and totally committed to the target and future vision. As a team we did our best to get into the project, not out of it.

Many fears can come into play when leading a team – it doesn't matter if it's your first time or you're an old hand, if you're in the corporate space or an entrepreneur. Once you're in that position, you transition from being the bright, eager person with a brilliant idea to a leader, manager, someone who people look to for inspiration. Sometimes this can happen more quickly than you can anticipate or even by accident.

Whatever the eventually, you must be prepared to handle the inevitable challenges.
The fear is real, but the good news is that the reasons for your fear can be overcome. These are the main fears I have faced as a leader and what I did to overcome them.

Fear of criticism – Most people do not enjoy nor want to be criticized but being a leader walks hand in hand with criticism and is an evitable part of being a leader. People will delight in highlighting your shortcomings which will take precedence over your strengths. The team you lead looks to you to make the right decisions and most people understand that no one is perfect, but they'll still have an opinion on your abilities. And if you're in public facing role, look forward to criticism from complete strangers. So, points to get you through it;

1. *Know that anything worth doing attracts admiration and criticism* – It's a choice of would you rather be judged or ignored? For example, I had to execute a major company restructuring with people losing roles, I approached the process knowing that for a while I'd be unpopular and that taking on some criticism was expected and acceptable. To make a noticeable difference, you going to have to dodge a few stones. It doesn't seem fair that what others risk by criticizing you or your actions, is miniscule compared to what you risk by putting yourself out there. A little reminder here, no one said it was fair and it should never stop you from being the right leader.

2. *Look criticism dead in the eye* – Adopting a criticism avoidance strategy is more damaging than you might realize. Being seen to avoid criticism is what makes you appear weaker, not the criticism itself. Don't let your fear of criticism outweigh your desire for success. Face the fear head on by regularly requesting feedback from your team either via 360-degree reviews or surveys with specific questions about how effective you are in your role - simply ask "How am I doing?

What else could I do to be a more impactful leader for this team?" Humility goes a long way.

3. *Look for improvement, not approval* – Like it or not there may be valuable insight cradling criticism, so instead of steering away from it, consider what is constructive. Find the titbit of truth in it and allow it to elevate you to higher standards. Think of it as exposing new self-discoveries.

4. *Ponder the intent of the criticism* – Is it intended to help you or hurt you? Identifying it as a source of support can be liberating. If it's the not so, but remember such criticism is often more about the other person than you. That person may be projecting his or her own fears or inadequacies. For the hybrid situation where it's meant to be helpful but isn't, view the criticism as merely giving you information about the inclinations and perspective of the provider. If it's really unpleasant I'd go back to a saying of my mum's "Empty vessel's, make the most noise."

5. *If you can't control the sting, keep it from burning* – No matter how strong we are, that initial moment when we're receiving criticism can still burn. How you react from that moment can mean the difference between the sting persisting and burning or quickly abating. The key is not to be overemotional or to overreact. Most often, the criticism is not meant to be a personal attack; it's not about you, it's about your work or your behavior. Key to remember is that, you control the pain from criticism - You can't change the words that were said to you, but you can change the meaning you attach to them.

6. *Decide who gets to criticize you* - Not all criticizers are created equal, and some shouldn't even have your ear. Set the criteria for those whose feedback matters and mentally dismiss the rest.

Fear of Failure – Failure sucks - especially when all eyes are on you. Driven people hate failure more than anything in the world. But you don't become a successful leader without having tasted failure along the way. Unfortunately, this is how most of us gain wisdom. We get presented with many opportunities to fail when we lead a team - making bad strategic decisions. Hiring the wrong people. Overpromising and under delivering. Not properly communicating the organizational vision and everyone's role in its success. There's no shortage of chances to fail but your response is telling. When you make mistakes, own them and let the team know what you are going to do starting today to put things right. It's not about failure; it's about learning and focusing on "failing forward." That is seek and accept feedback from failures ensuring that you turn them into positive lessons to guide your future success.

Fear of Decision - Making – There is nothing more paralyzing for a team than an indecisive leader. It doesn't always have to be the right decision, sometimes it's just about making a decision and moving forward. Analysis paralysis can cripple an organization you might make the wrong decision but just refer back to the handling failure section. Having worked in a fast-moving environment, the ability to make good decisions quickly can be all you need to take your business to the next level. And this may seem like a contradiction but sometimes you have to slow down and take your time, even if it means missing a great opportunity. To find your balance, you need to practice decision making;

1. Adopt a habit of daily decision making both important and not so important decisions that will help you progress toward your goals and see the impact.

2. Take actions after you made your decision that way you'll know if your decision was right or wrong a lot sooner and overcome your fear of making the wrong decisions.

3. Increase your confidence in decision making by having as much pertinent information to hand as possible to shape your decision and reduce the probability of making the wrong decision.
4. If your decision was wrong, learn from your mistakes. If your decision was right, what made it successful and how could you improve?
5. Motivate yourself to make the right decision. Question yourself before you decide to decide, use cost and benefit analyses to weight pros and cons of each decision. Think through what could be the worst and best outcomes if you make a decision and if you don't make a decision. What do you need to do if things go wrong?

Fear of Speaking - The fear of public speaking always seems top people's phobias but as a leader within an organization, one of the things you should be doing the most is publicly addressing your team. Your team likes to know that you have everything under control, when bad news has to be delivered they want to hear from someone they know, not by a remote boss or email. If you can't do this with confidence, then how can you expect your team to follow you into "battle?" My recommendation is to take every opportunity you can to speak in front of audiences. This could be during meetings, in client presentations, toastmasters or similar, or speaking at industry conferences. Practice makes perfect. The more you do it, the more confident you will be. Don't aim for perfection — your team will actually love imperfection more – you're human! Be yourself and embrace the fear. It means you're alive.

Fear of Responsibility – To quote Spiderman "With great power comes great responsibility" and you cannot expect to be a leader without it. The leadership role comes laden with responsibilities; you're not just responsible to clients, the Board and shareholders but your team too – who should be your main priority. If you put them first, all the rest will fall into place. As a leader your role is to define the goal, provide direction and resources, and remove obstacles. Embrace the fact that you have a team to lead. It's a good problem to have. Assuming you have the right people in the right roles and you're looking out for their best interests, they can be your best resource for important information. Keep them in the loop as much as feasibly possible and they'll have no problem reciprocating same. Working together as a team will lighten that burden of responsibility.

Fear of Being Unpopular – Being a leader is not a popularity contest and you can't be all things to all men or women. If you've been promoted from within the ranks, there may be growing pains from your former peer group. You may be the one who "changed" now that you are in management. It's a common problem. Remember, always, that you're supposed to be in this role. Your old peers may not see it, but there have been few promotions where everyone in the company agreed with it. If subordinates are complaining, there is likely a need buried in there and most likely not with you, you're just a new ear to end. Face them head on and ask them, specifically, what they want. What can you do to make it work? If you don't call it out, the team may inadvertently sabotage the decisions that are going to be made. Calling it out shows that you're in control and that you want to hear what they have to say.

Fear of Not Knowing Enough to Be a Leader – Good old impostor syndrome! Trust yourself, I've not come across many businesses that appoint a leader to fail. If you've achieved an internal promotion, then your organization has acknowledged that you have earned a seat at the table. Look at logically, think of all the hoops you jumped through for interview, how many years you've worked in organization/industry, the learning you may have undertaken. You're not there by fluke, you're there because you rightfully earned it. Don't let a fear of not knowing enough, hold you back from fulfilling your leadership potential.

These are just a few of the fears that come with leadership. Each of us will have to face fear at some time or another. Whatever your fear is, it's always best to face it head on. So, here's what I'd say to any woman who finds the thought of professional power less than appealing. Just try it. Yes, from where you're standing now it may seem terrifying or just plain unappealing or even limiting, but once you get a taste of it, there's more than a good chance you'll see how sweet it is. And if it doesn't suit you or you feel it undermines your other goals, you can still walk away. I did, but that's another story!

This woman can self-reflection questions;

- If you're not leader – what's stopping, you?
- What actions can you take to overcome your fears?

"I've learned that fear limits you and your vision. It serves as blinders to what may be just a few steps down the road for you. The journey is valuable, but believing in your talents, your abilities, and your self-worth can empower you to walk down an even brighter path. Transforming fear into freedom - how great is that?"
Soledad O'Brien

19. This Woman Can... have a courageous conversation!

Working as a senior executive can be a lonely job. You have to deliver tough messages and most everyone I know dreads the difficult, challenging conversation. This includes conversations in which we have to deliver unpleasant news, discuss a delicate subject, or talk about something that needs to change or has gone wrong. Then conversely there are times we can't talk at all and have to keep key decisions confidential until the timing is right.

I've had to deliver grim messages to people I've considered friends around job losses, dismissals and during disciplinary hearings – just the thought of having those conversations— whether with your partner, children, relatives, friends, or colleagues can make you anxious and filled with trepidation. It plays on your mind, taking up space and distracting you from other important considerations that need your attention.

You become more concerned about the reaction of the recipient and how uncomfortable you'll feel in the situation rather than the message you need to deliver. Because of this you procrastinate in their delivery, doing everything in your power to avoid having them altogether. Relax, such discomfort is natural and normal but the problem with avoidance is that, unless the situation resolves itself, putting it off only allows it to continue and potentially get worse.

Whilst it doesn't get any more comfortable delivering the message it can get easier with planning and preparation. These two factors can help turn down the volume of your apprehension and make it much more likely that the difficult conversations you need to have will be successful.

Preparation

For challenging or difficult topics, it's wise to plan in advance when you'll have the conversation, no one likes to be blindsided. It can be as simple as "I'd like to talk with you about..." or "We really need to talk about..." Then, agree on a time and a place for the conversation, make sure there's enough space for all participants to be "comfortable enough" and to see each other clearly especially if it's a group message.

If it's more of a performance related topic, it's never helpful to collect and hold on to feelings of frustration, anger, or resentment for days, weeks, or longer and then unload all these feelings on another person all at once. Whenever possible, attempt to discuss challenging issues as they come up or soon thereafter.

There are some key ground rules;

- Know the objective you want to accomplish with the conversation? What is the desired outcome? What are the non-negotiables? What are the objectives you want to achieve by the end of the conversation? Once you have determined this, plan how you will close the conversation. Don't end without clearly expressed action items. What is the person agreeing to do? What support are you committed to provide? What obstacles might prevent these remedial actions from taking place? What do you both agree to do to overcome potential obstacles? Schedule a follow up to evaluate progress and definitively reach closure on the issue at hand.
- Whenever possible, stay at about the same eye level - everyone participating should be either seated or

standing. It's generally not helpful for one person to be physically "above" or "below" others.

- Speak directly to the other person(s).

- Speak as calmly in an as even a voice as possible. This maximizes the chances that others will hear the content of your message and not be fixated on your emotions. They're already tense just attending the meeting.

- If you're in a one to one setting, don't point fingers, this is not a time to be apportioning blame. This just tends to put the other person in defensive mode or that he or she is being lectured or put down.

- I've been in meetings where the boss has been pretty derogatory, not just to the people in the room but including people not attendance – avoid this at all costs. Name-calling, shouting, screaming, cursing, put-downs, insults, or threats (emotional or physical) have no place in delivering a message – no matter how upset or impacted you are – it's not about you. When any of these happen, the only thing other people hear is anger and attack. As a result, they are likely to leave, shut down or attack as well. Treating others with respect is essential to healthy communication.

- Spend some time describing your concerns and the things you'd like to happen differently, being as clear as possible using specific examples. Avoid the use of the words "always," "never," "everything," and "nothing." They may express your frustration and upset, but they overgeneralize and are fundamentally inaccurate and play no part in the communication process.

- Once you've delivered your message, allow the recipients to respond without interruption. More importantly, when they are speaking, consciously listen to what he or she has to say with the intent of hearing it. This is very different from waiting for the other person to finish speaking so you can respond. If you're thinking about what you're going to say in response, while he or she is still speaking, you're not listening. Conversely, there may be moments in the conversation where a silence occurs. It's at these points you may get uncomfortable, but silence is golden. Don't rush to fill it with words, take the time to hear what has been said and let the message sink in, it can help you connect better and lead to a better outcome. So, embrace the pauses.

- Make sure you understand what the other person has said before you respond. Ask for clarification, if you're unsure what he or she said or meant. "Could you please repeat that?" "I'm not sure what you mean. Can you please help me better understand?"

- Approach the conversation with openness and an interest in problem solving, rather than needing to be "right." It's not a competition where we need to be "right," and the other person has to be "wrong." This kind of rigid either-or, win-lose, or right-wrong mindset makes conflict much more likely and mutual understanding much less likely.

- If your conversation is performance related rather than a general communication - part of your preparation should involve you asking yourself two important questions: "What exactly is the behavior that is causing the problem?" and "What is the impact that the behavior is having on you, the team or the organization?" You need to be clear on this for yourself, so you can articulate the issue in two or three succinct statements. If not, you risk going off on a tangent during the conversation. The lack of focus on the central issue will derail the conversation and sabotage your intentions.

- In a group situation, stick to the topic at hand and focus on the topic of this conversation. Bringing up issues or complaints related to other topics or past events just blurs the message you're trying to deliver and interferes with healthy communication during the conversation. Park those other issues for another time, if they're important to you, you'll remember them.

- Do not walk away or leave the conversation without the other person's agreement. Allow for the possibility of time-outs. It's important to discuss and mutually agree to the concept of a "time-out" as needed. Time-outs are not just for young children or professional sports teams. If things start to become too heated, it's important for people to be able to take a time-out. Time-outs give people the opportunity and the space to calm down and compose themselves, making it possible to continue.

- Take responsibility for feeling the way you do, rather than blaming the meeting attendees. No one can make you feel a specific way, you're in charge of your emotions and reactions. Use "I" statements — as in, "I feel..." Be clear and specific about what the other person did that contributed to your reaction. Rather than saying, "You make me so mad," focus on the other person's actual behaviors.

- Lose your assumptions. Just because you've known individuals for a period of time, it doesn't mean you know what the other person is feeling or thinking. Spend a little time to reflect on your attitude toward the situation and the person involved. What are your preconceived notions about it? Your mindset will predetermine your reaction and interpretations of the other person's responses, so it pays to approach such conversations with an open mindset. Be prepared to hear first what the other parties have to say before reaching conclusions. Even if you think the topic is an open and shut situation. People grow and change. What you want, need, or expect from each other changes and may need to be renegotiated from time to time remain open in all situations.

- Nobody wants to hear unpleasant news and so the reaction you receive on delivery may across as confrontational. Most times, this is rarely personal so don't take it that way. We're never 100% sure of the coping mechanisms of team members and how they'll handle bad news. You need to develop your conflict resolution skills. It's a natural part of human interaction and managing conflict effectively is one of the vital skills of leadership. Have a few, proven phrases that can come in handy in crucial spots.

- Another coping mechanism manifests itself in thwarting ploys. This is when the recipient responds in tactics such as stonewalling, sarcasm and accusing. It's uncomfortable but again it's your job to recognize and simply address the ploy openly and sincerely. For example, if the ploy from your counterpart is to be stubbornly unresponsive to questions, you can frankly say, "I don't know how to interpret your silence." Disarm the ploy by labeling the observed behavior.

Ultimately, you cannot control how the other person(s) will react to your efforts to engage them in challenging but necessary conversations. However, by being well prepared, authentic and respectful in your approach, it maximizes the chances of your conversation serving its intended purpose.

This woman can self-reflection questions;

- What conversations do you struggle with?
- How can you be better prepared the next time you have a courageous conversation?

"Be brave enough to start a conversation that matters."
Margaret Wheatley

20. This Woman Can... integrate life and work!

On my rise through the heady ranks of senior leadership I can honestly say that I never focused on becoming a CEO – my sole focus was trying to hold down a job, study for my degrees whilst single handedly raising two boys and retain some level of sanity in the mix. What the hell was work-life balance? I may be showing my age, but I don't think that was ever a thing. As an ambitious woman trying to put food on the table I only knew I had to find a way to make it all work. A typical day for you probably looks like this: You're working on that report, but you have to leave the office early because you have to take child number one to the dentist. You're trying to get dinner on the table when an important client email comes in, and next thing you know the kids are screaming that they're hungry and you have to order take-away for dinner. You forfeit your quarterly hair appointment to attend a parent – teacher meeting and you still have to complete that report! I'm sure you can insert your own scenario and a day that doesn't go quite to plan.

Thirty years after embarking on my career I still see exactly the same challenges for working women – even Serena Williams being one of the world's most successful athletes still has to deal with the challenges that working mums have had to tackle since forever. My kids are grown but I can hear the saying – "the more things change, the more they stay the same"

Maybe you're starting your career, wondering how to find that elusive work-life balance or maybe you're knee in your career and still haven't figured out your magic formula. I found the family and career INTEGRATION not balance I needed—even in a leadership position. So, I wanted to share, both what has worked for me and the strategies utilized by the many women I've coached;

Adopt a work-life integration mindset – Top of the list is to forget the notion of trying to create a balance, it's near on impossible to avoid work and life merging into one, so you might as well make the most of it and align your goals to create the life experience you want. For the most part, the boundaries that used to exist between our work and personal lives have blurred meaning quite often work is life and life is work. Get your mind into that space to gain some perspective, this isn't just a job you're working, this is your life that you're building. You don't have time to be around people who bring you down or to work for a company you don't love, so be selective with your employer and your friends to avoid wasting valuable time.

Strengthen your skills, to increase your leverage in the workplace – Maybe you want to work from home one day a week. Is that really going to be a problem if everyone knows you're extremely good at what you do? Start thinking about what you can do to build your skills and gain more leverage. You may not benefit from it straight away, but it will increase your value in the job market and help gain the work-life integration you want down the road.

Optimize your day – Some of us are morning people, some of us are night owls, each day presents its own unique challenges and opportunities, but you have to find ways to make your day more efficient and productive if you want to leave work at work. I'm at my best in the mornings – I can slay dragons and move mountains, but my client Carrie is the total opposite. She takes time at the end of her work day prepping everything she needs for the next day. She puts it all in place because she's lethargic when she gets to work in the morning. This pre-day prep allows her to do the minimum in the morning until she's completely awake and alert.

Be clear on your priorities – You can't do it all, no matter your best intentions. Focus on the key components that you want to get to in your days, whether it's fitness, self-care, meals with the family, and schedule them on your calendar at a regular cadence. Treat them with the seriousness you bring to meetings and deadlines at work.

Use your vacation days for vacation - I say this gingerly because I always found it difficult to use holidays for holiday until I experienced a burn out episode, I learnt the hard way to respect my time off – if you can't achieve everything at least focus on achieving 1 or 2 points

- *Don't work on holidays – or at least have rules* – When I travelled especially in a different time zone I would receive calls and emails at all times of the night. So, I let everyone know that I'd top and tail my day answering at specific times in the morning and evening. That message would be on my out of office notification and my call answering service.

- *Don't take the pay* – Stop rolling over vacation days. Even if your company allows it, make it a point to use them every year, even if you don't go anywhere. A quiet staycation can be just as restorative as a trip to the beach. I made a habit of periodically checking holiday usage and enforced the use or lose it vacation policy making sure everyone knew they were throwing money away if they take a break.

- *Schedule in Some 3-Day Weekends* – If you really feel you can't take a long break, schedule regular 3-day weekends during those very few yearly holidays? Every few months, schedule your own mini-vacation by taking off a Friday or a Monday. Make an escape or simply enjoy being at home, it will give you something to look forward to and help you get your head back on track so you're doing your best work once you return.

Don't fall at the first hurdle – Recognize that developing the right integration habit is a process and takes time to settle in. Be prepared to adapt as to go, it's an evolution you'll always be tweaking and adjusting, and you'll probably constantly feel like you're not getting the ratios right, but as with any good recipe, it tends to work out when it all comes together.

You're not Superwoman – If you are overwhelmed at work, and it is causing undue stress don't suffer in silence. Shed the Superwoman image and explain your situation to your boss or supervisor. Untenable work situations can usually be alleviated, but it will take some assertiveness on your part. Take advantage of the services offered by your employee assistance program.

Give yourself permission –Things go wrong, your day can be unpredictable from the time you wake up, not enough milk for cereal, unfinished homework, early kid pick up so you miss a work deadline, you get the idea. The best advice I can come up with is: be flexible, lower your expectations, laugh at yourself, be present, and try to enjoy the little moments.

Compartmentalizing is Key – It all comes down to compartmentalizing and not being ashamed to ask for help. It's important to be a professional and a good mother, but it's important to be present in both roles, instead of stressing about failing someone all of the time. When I was with my boys, I focused on time with them, eventually they got fed up of me and wanted their own space, but it was time totally focused on them – at the park, reading, building sheet tents or creating our own cinema nights with DVDs and popcorn. No work, no computer, no distractions, 100% mum and sons time. When I hit work, I closed all of my internet browsers and put my cell phone in my desk drawer until I need it for something work-related, focus on what I was paid to do – get it done and I could hopefully finish on time.

Sometimes it was difficult, but I felt so much better at being a wife/mom/worker when I was fully present in the moment, instead of trying to multitask more than necessary."

Don't Be a Martyr – This is tough, we pride ourselves on getting things done with minimal support, how many times have you been offered help and your response is "I got this?" when really, you'd love the support. As women we need to stop glorifying being a martyr for their family. We need to take care of ourselves in order to do the very best for our children. If help is offered take it, if you can use extended family to help you out, use it – this is what I found is the most effective way to juggle being a mother, business owner, employee, and still have a happy life. If you can afford it, pay for help – send out your laundry, hire someone to come clean up your house, having that extra time will be super beneficial to your well-being — even if it just means allowing you to take a nap or watch a funny movie. At some point, you're going to realize you can't do it all — no one can. Because of that, it's important to ask others for help when you need it.

Find your Support Network – Surround yourself with others that are like-minded. Ideally not from work as your brain will automatically switch into work mode, If that's not possible it's still invaluable to have other women that know what you're going through, can cheer you on, give tips and tricks, and to just be an ear to listen to complaints and tears. Without that support, it would be very difficult to do all that we need to do as working women in one of our most important jobs of being a mom. As a single parent, my best friend, sister and I used to club together for holidays (it was cheaper to rent a larger apartment and split the costs than going individually). We'd take turns to babysit so one of us could get a break, those few hours were a lifesaver when you were a frazzled mum.

It's all about you! – When we're busy making sure that employees, the boss, colleagues, our partner and children, it can be so easy for the most important person (aka you) to be pushed aside, relegated in the priority ranking, so get into the habit of scheduling Me-Time put you first. Self-care isn't selfish, its self-preservation.

- *Get some sleep* – Unless you work shifts, you may be unable to change the fact that work begins at 8am or 9am, so avoid the late nights and ensure that you get your regular seven hours of sleep every night. This will also help you make full use of your time in the office, reducing the need to work past office hours.

- *Exercise* – Don't underestimate the power of exercise. It's not just about getting in shape, but maintaining your health, improving mental acuity and your self-esteem too. Don't limit yourself to just going to the gym – go for a swim or a dance class, something that makes you move at least once a week.

- *Get a hobby* – One not work-related as it can help you feel more purposeful outside of your work goals.

- *Relieve your stress* – Working constantly can leave you frazzled and stress you out. To avoid that negativity seeping into your home life, find something that helps you relieve your stress —a morning meditation or a lunchtime walk.

- *Take your lunch breaks* – I know it can be easier said than done but eating a salad in front of your computer isn't a break. It's still working, just while shoveling food into your mouth. Make a point to leave work during your lunch break, whether it's to meet a friend at a restaurant, take a walk, browse a favorite store or just read a book on a park bench. I scheduled lunch breaks in my online work diary, marked as private and arranged meetings around them. I chose whether to forfeit my break and people trying to book meetings would see me as unavailable and schedule accordingly.

Don't be afraid to clear your schedule – Sometimes you just need a little "me" time, and that means clearing everything you can off your schedule, so you can actually devote some moments of peace to yourself. Sure, you'll feel guilty but ask yourself, how many times have you changed your personal schedule to devote extra time to work? If you have a role that allows it, take a longer lunch to do something that makes you feel good. I know we always feel like we're playing hooky from school when doing personal activities in work time but how come we don't feel guilty doing work activity during our personal time?

The overall goal is to get the work done, how and when you do it should be a lesser concern.

Control the beast called Work!

- *Pay attention to how many hours you work* – Some days are so jam-packed that it's hard to even find the slightest bit of time for yourself, and that's OK — there are only 24 hours in a day, after all. But if you're constantly working more hours than you can count, that's a problem. You may look like a hero but your productivity dips as you work longer so you're defeating the objective of being at work!
- *Handle that phone situation* – Stop constantly checking your emails, put your phone on airplane mode once you leave the office for the day, that way you won't get any emails, calls, messages, or alerts from anyone at work and can get some major head space in the process. Same goes for instant messaging. I often quote my first experience with a company Blackberry phone. It blinked red every time an email landed which was often from my boss. As I'd just started in the role I felt obligated to answer, the problem was he was a

micro manager, so I'd fall asleep to a blinking red light and woke up to a blinking red light. During one of my reviews I felt compelled to discuss how the constant emailing made me feel – that I felt like I went to bed with him and woke with him, but he wasn't my husband! He was totally oblivious to the volume of messages and we agreed a way forward.

- *Don't give out your personal number* – If possible have a separate number for work to allow you to switch off but enable your VIPs to contact you if needed. Don't give out your personal number. Once you open that door, you're bound to receive emails and calls from your boss and employees after-hours on a regular basis.

- *Keep your weekends work-free* – This goes hand in hand with my initial point, you've probably put in a load of hours during the week, so why log even more on the weekends if you don't have to? Sure, it can be nice using your days off to get ahead. The only problem with that is it's taking time away from yourself, and when you're (literally) working 24/7, that's a fast-track to burnout. Instead, vow to save Saturday and Sunday to reenergize yourself — no work emails allowed. When Monday rolls around, you'll be glad you got a nice break.

Identify a work area at home and stick to it – Working from home can often seem like the answer to all our challenges – think about it, you can be taking client calls, answering your boss' emails, playing video games with the kids, put on a load of washing and cooking dinner all at once – that's the reality! We all know how multi-talented we are, but this is one area where you shouldn't blur the lines. The scenarios I described can present you even more challenges, if you don't have a certain area of your home designated to working — one you can walk away from and not return to until you mean business again — you'll end up working all the time. Multi-tasking means you don't give one activity 100% attention which can be detrimental – each task takes longer to complete, you're not focused so mistakes can occur and if kids are involved they're not getting quality time with you and before you know it, you're still working at 11pm and you start to associate all that stress that comes from your job with your home, making it hard to escape and truly relax. So, play smart, find a spot at home you can work, negotiate with the kids to give you an hour uninterrupted time to allow you finish that report, be strict with emails by only checking emails on the hour, have a mental clocking off time so you do actually stop working.

Don't live too close to work – I've experienced both extremes of work – home proximity. I had a role that presented me with a daily 160-mile return commute in the UK and when I moved to the Caribbean that commute became less than two miles. I thought that would be a dream – I could choose to have a lie in or exercise and still make it to my desk on time, but the downside was that I was incredibly accessible, so it was no problem for my boss to call a last minute meeting at the end of the day or request a weekend meeting, as a key holder when others needed access it was easier to come to my home for a key and I'd think nothing of popping into the office on the weekend to catch up. Then I realized I missed my long commute – this was the time I caught up on phone calls with friends, listened to audiobooks etc. with minimum interruption- it was my Me-time! When I needed some space, it was impossible to get it: I could be walking outside and bump into co-workers or clients which in the case of the latter invariably ended in a work-related conversation regarding issues they never knew they had until they saw you and required your urgent attention. Sometimes just seeing the office building in the distance caused me to switch into office mode. When there's physical distance between your home and your workplace, it's easier to rid your job from your mind until it's time to go back.

Clarify the difference between "urgent" and "important" – As much as we try to control them, certain circumstances will require us to disregard the whole concept of segregating work and home. In those cases, try to identify which errands require your attention now (these matters are "urgent") versus which things carry weight but are not pressing (these are "important"). Matters which are both "urgent" and "important" will be the ones you need to attend to first. It's also worth clarifying the same with your Boss, how many times have you received a weekend email, dropped everything to address it and your Boss replies "Thanks but it could have waited until Monday!"

Leave Work at Work – I mentioned the main upside of my long commute earlier which demonstrated the advantage of developing a mental on-off switch between work and home and whilst a long commute isn't your solution, establish one that works for you. It might consist of listening to music or audiobooks on your drive home, a fitness class after work, running, cycling or walking home, running errands or keeping personal appointments. Scheduling such activities immediately after work hours also prevents you from spending that extra ten minutes at the office which then morphs into several hours.

Many hands make light work – Try as we might home, and family related tasks still fall resoundingly into a woman's lap, but it doesn't mean that daddy can't get in on the act. A working mom has a lot to juggle and it's their right to ask daddy to should some of the responsibility. Between you, figure out how your spouse can get involved in childcare after all it took two make a baby and it doesn't stop there! Maybe he shares the school run, takes them swimming or does the bedtime ritual. If you work best at different hours, bag night-time for yourself and let him have the early hours. More time together can only improve their bonding and give you some time off!

Be flexible – despite our best plans, it doesn't mean that you will achieve it 100% of the time. What it does mean however, is that you are conscious of the times that you haven choose to substitute your me time for other things. The important thing is to remember that when you choose to substitute that it's the exception as opposed to the rule. Having an awareness and understanding of where you are willing and want to spend your time to create your work-life blend makes you feel more personally and professionally fulfilled.

Finding work-life integration that works for you may not be easy but is definitely worth the effort. Progressing in our career is made all the more difficult if we don't look after ourselves, mentally and physically. Remember, if you don't design a career that you love, someone else will do it for you. And you may not like their version.

This woman can self-reflection questions;

- How do you currently practice self-care?
- What would make the biggest difference to you achieving work life integration?

"Women, in particular, need to keep an eye on their physical and mental health, because if we're scurrying to and from appointments and errands, we don't have a lot of time to take care of ourselves. We need to do a better job of putting ourselves higher on our own 'to do' list."
Michelle Obama

21. This Woman Can... proactively support other women.

Valerie had recently been promoted to VP of Marketing, a well-deserved role but she was butting heads with a few of her female team members. She had overheard a female colleague describing her as a bitch and stating how much she'd changed since she'd got the position "Who did she think she was? I didn't think she'd be like this. I thought having a woman as a boss would be different, it feels like we've just swapped our old VP for a man in a skirt"

Valerie was devastated, she'd worked really hard to get her position and yes, she was going to make sure that no-one took her role. "I've had to work hard to get here, why can't they respect that and let me get on with my job?"
Valerie had developed a case of the Queen Bee syndrome - the notion that there can only be one woman at the top and because of this she had to "defend' her position.

I've met some unpleasant female leaders and I'm happy to say I've been fortunate to have not been led by them. I could never understand the stance they'd taken, as far as I was concerned if I delivered my job to the best of my capabilities, I had nothing to fear. However, having worked across a number of industries I have also observed that some women feel compelled to change who they are to either fit in with their male counterparts or assert their authority as they fear they won't be respected if they are themselves. I get it, our levels of self-confidence can vary depending on the situation and shoves us into leadership survival mode but that just perpetuates the

Queen Bee syndrome and I can appreciate why some women get a bad rap because like Valerie, they're not really showing up in their best light.

So, when it comes to female leadership, I think we have to look at it from both sides of the coin;

- If you work with a female leader, we need to respect the journey, put ourselves in the female leader's proverbial shoes, and take learnings to either emulate or improve if you aspire to achieve same.

And

- If you are a female leader, you should be secure in the role, you've earned your seat at the table, I'm sure no-one gave it to you. Respect and credibility comes with how you treat people – it's not an automatic right with the job title. Your role would be easier to execute, if you weren't looking over your shoulder wondering who was going to topple you from your perch. If you're doing what you were hired to do to the best of your capabilities, then you don't need the burden of the additional stress trying to protect your position.
- There's room at the top for all of us!

The myth that there can only be room at the top for one woman has been highly perpetrated over the years - think of all the rivalries

- Beyoncé v Rihanna
- Bette Davis v Joan Crawford
- Cardi B v Nicki Minaj
- Nancy Kerrigan v Tonya Harding
- Mary J v Faith Evans
- Venus Williams v Serena Williams

TV continues to push the message that successful women can't get along, the whole Real Housewives franchise is based on this premise, plus countless others all pushing the catfights, warring women, bitchy, gossip hounds and mean girl cliques. The unfortunate point is that the attitude portrayed and encouraged by the media for ratings is incredibly damaging for those of us who do work in the real world and not reality TV. This translates into the workplace as an assertive woman being labeled "bossy" or a "ball buster", women who disagree amongst themselves classed as being in a catfight, our often-valid concerns dismissed as over reactions or trivial jealousies. All very damaging and invalid, women are no more likely to fight in the workplace than a man, our decision making isn't flawed because we don't have a dangling appendage!

Don't get me wrong, it's not all media's fault, we as women have a part to play especially if we've already made it to the top;

- We fought hard to get to where we are and probably even harder to remain at the top – nobody helped us get there and we sure as dammit won't let any young and upwardly mobile upstart take our spot without a fight!
- On the same front we expect women to help us just because they are a woman. We expect that should be prepared to sacrifice opportunities and success to let another woman get a foot on the ladder, not because the woman earned it.
- An insecure woman, one who isn't secure in who she is and what she can offer and deliver in business or life, will inevitably feel that every other woman is a potential threat to her ultimate success and make sure another woman doesn't even see the ladder let alone get her foot on it.

You don't see these portrayals amongst men. Who's the best yes, but not that only one man can rule at a time, so why is it so prevalent for women and how can we push those negative stereotypes aside?

At the core we should acknowledge that your female colleague is your best asset and ally and we should be supporting each, not tearing each other down.

Stop the popularity contest - Women face the double bind standard that men don't. Men are expected to be assertive and confident, and are seen as leaders, whereas, women are expected to be nurturing and collaborative. When we are assertive and lead we can be deemed unlikable as that's not how a woman is supposed to act. So we often face pushback from men and women described "pushy" "ambitious" or my favorite "over-confident" as opposed to a man being "forthright" and "strong."

When you hear a woman being called "bossy" or "a nag," ask for a specific example of what the woman did and then ask, "Would you have the same reaction if a man did the same thing?" Most times, the answer will be no. When you're having a negative response to a woman at work, ask yourself the same question and give her the benefit of the doubt. Chances are she's just doing her job.

Bring them with you - If you've been fortunate to move up the ladder, look at the pool of women in your network and see who could complement you on this opportunity — and also help advance their career.

Surround yourself with the best and utilize them! - Your colleagues are an asset to you – but you have to let them be. You have to be willing to step back when they know better than you do; you have to be ready to ask for help and dismiss the idea it makes you look weak. In my opinion the strength is in asking for support; you have the confidence to step forward and acknowledge what you don't know.

Identify excellence in others - Women are often given less credit for a job well done and are more likely to be singled out for failure. But we also respond in different ways – women will put success down to external factors such as "good luck" and "help from the team," while men will beat their chest and claim the victory as theirs and it's all down to the skills and abilities. Men own success women undermine theirs and if we do celebrate our success we seen as braggadocios or big headed or self-promoting.

If you see a job well done by a woman, acknowledge it, if you see a woman being unfairly for a mistake point it out. Even better, take time to celebrate one another's successes whenever possible, there's nothing to stop us uplifting our colleagues for a job well done. If you have the opportunity to introduce a female colleague, highlight their credentials and accomplishments—for example, "Trina was in charge of our new sales team and they've have the best performance all year"

Encourage Women to Go for It - We all know that as women, we suffer from self-doubt all the time. We have to 100% of everything before we make a move, whilst a man only needs to know he has 60% of the criteria before making his move. We know it's unfortunately still a man's world and we have to work extra hard to prove our capabilities and it doesn't help when we undermine our own performance and ability further eroding our confidence.

So, if you see an opportunity you know your colleague is a shoe in for, boost her confidence and encourage them to go for it. If she says she's not ready for a new project or role, remind her of how far she has come, what she's already accomplished and offer to be a sounding board whilst she gets up to speed.

Recognizing excellence in other women and in yourself is the task and the strength of supporting women.

Be flattered not threatened - If you hear word that someone's coming for your job, you really shouldn't be worried – you know what you did to get there, and you know what to do to remain – no need to be insecure in your abilities. On the contrary, give the individual some insight into your world – we all know it's easier to do the job with your feet on couch than walking a mile in your heels. Personally, I've never been threatened by this situation I see it as a great opportunity to impart my knowledge, after all I already my eyes focused on the next prize.

Be your own fabulous self - Lead by example and be your own authentic, fabulous, self! If you're waffling about whether to speak up in a meeting, just say some something. If you're not sure if you should wear that insane outfit you bought, just wear it. Every time you show your opinion or your personal style confidently, you signal to other women that it's okay to be themselves. We women are all diverse and unique. Everyone will have different skills and bring different flavors to the table—there shouldn't be one template that all women in the workplace are shooting to achieve, then we'd all beige and boring!

Give women direct feedback - Don't just praise, look for opportunities to give the women you work with input that can help them learn and grow. Holding back for fear you'll upset someone doesn't benefit her, if should be constructive and relevant and whenever possible, live and in the moment to be most effective. If on the receiving end you should treat feedback as a gift and solicit it often—you'll benefit from the input.

Ensure women are heard - Next time you're in a meeting, look at the seating placements. Most men will see at the front or middle whilst women tend to take less powerful positions such as the end of the table and it can often be a situation of who talks loudest often gets heard – normally a male!

Start sitting front-and-center and speaking up in meetings, encourage other women to do the same. If a woman is interrupted, interject and say you'd like to hear her finish. When a co-worker runs away with a woman's idea, remind everyone whose idea it was by saying, "Great idea . . . thanks to Trina for suggesting it." Proactively seek ways to hear the opinions of others such going around the room soliciting feedback, points raised by other women. When you advocate for your female colleagues, they benefit—and you're also seen as a leader plus meetings are far more effective when everyone's point is heard

Blowing out someone else's candle doesn't make yours shine any brighter. Strong women stand together when things are rough, hold each other up when they need support and laugh together when there's no reason to. Be that woman! By not competing, learning to control our reactions and pushing back against prejudice, everyone stands to benefit. There's room at the top for everyone.

This woman can self-reflection questions;

- If you are a leader, how are you championing women within your organization?
- If you are a subordinate, how can you take the initiative to work with women in senior positions?

"Women need to support other women, and we must ensure we are providing women with opportunities that allow them to reach their full potential."
Whitney Wolfe Herd

About the Author

Janice Sutherland is the Caribbean's top women's leadership expert, executive coach and podcast host. Through leadership training and elite-level mentorship, she coaches women around the world to take their rightful seat at the tables where the important decisions are made. From being a single parent of two with zero qualifications, Janice rose through the ranks securing senior executive roles with prestigious multi-nationals even crossing continents to become the first female CEO for the Caribbean's leading Communications and Entertainment provider. Her belief in that nothing is insurmountable once you adopt the right mindset, coupled with her global leadership perspective makes Janice a leadership force to be reckoned with. Janice's unique background and passionate attitude allows her to inspire women to advance their careers and develop the confidence, presence and influence they need to drive through leadership barriers and confidently navigate the Board room.

Janice is a source of inspiration with her can do positive attitude. A true leader, she continuously coached those around her, not just her direct reports, but also her peers and her bosses. I cannot think anyone I could respect more as a leadership coach. Janice has done it all and therefore when she is coaching you it is from a place of experience. This lady has walked the walk and will help you achieve all that you set out to achieve.
Sarah Martin – Chief Executive Officer

If you look forward to an honest, fair, relevant yet fresh perspective of your reality, then I can't think of a more appropriate person to call on than Janice. I first met Janice,

as one of the first Caribbean women in a position of senior leadership in a space that was necessarily and significantly male dominated.... a position well-earned and one in which she thrived over the years! What is particularly endearing about Janice is the fact that behind the steely boss lady persona is the most down to earth Caribbean chick you would ever meet! While challenging us to confront behaviors which require improvement, Janice has the real-life material to offer solutions that are only practical and attainable. And she does it selflessly and unassumingly... making it look easy - although she would be quick to remind you that although the road to success should be fun, it certainly is no game! Through her own experiences, Janice has what it takes to offer good solutions to shorten the process of trial and error and to guide us to the most effective path to our own success...in whatever shape or form that might take. She has been there, she has done that, and she is the real deal!
Corinne Phillip - Legal and Regulatory Director

One of Janice's strongest assets is being able to look at the big picture yet focus on the areas where improvement is most needed on any given situation. As a leader, her coaching sessions were learning opportunities which provided positive reinforcement and a framework to push you to excel. A very "can do" attitude and solutions orientated leader. Janice strives to seek the right balance of careful listening with sharing her wealth of experience and ideas. She brings relevance and real-life experiences along with an excellent business acumen and savvy.
Terry-Ann Benjamin – HR Consultant and Managing Director

Janice is a force of nature and that is putting it mildly! Enthusiastic, driven, passionate about what she does, highly productive and ambitious - and that is just the tip of the iceberg. I love working with Janice because she inspires me. 'Prolific' is the word I used to describe her the most because she doesn't do anything by halves. Janice has transformed

from a very successful Telecoms CEO to a very successful entrepreneur, leadership consultant and coach. Her years of experience, charismatic personality and leadership skillset make her the only person you should consider if you are looking to develop your teams' leadership skills.
Dee Hutchinson – Best Selling Author and CEO

www.ingramcontent.com/pod-product-compliance
Lightning Source LLC
Chambersburg PA
CBHW070954240526
45469CB00016B/804